GETTING A JOB

resume writing,
job application letters,
and interview strategies

Barbara L. Croft

Merrill Publishing Company
A Bell & Howell Information Company
Columbus   Toronto   London   Melbourne

Published by Merrill Publishing Company
A Bell & Howell Information Company
Columbus, Ohio 43216

This book was set in Univers.

Administrative Editor: John Yarley
Production Coordinator: Linda Hillis Bayma
Cover Designer: Brian Deep

Library of Congress Catalog Card Number: 88-61782
International Standard Book Number: 0-675-20917-X
Printed in the United States of America
1 2 3 4 5 6 7 8 9—93 92 91 90 89

The names, addresses, and situations in this book are fictitious; they do not
represent real people or businesses. The author and publisher disclaim liability
incurred in connection with the use of the information in this book.

preface

Whether you're a top executive or a factory worker, a recent graduate or an experienced worker attempting to change careers, the job-search process is the same. It's a sales campaign, and you're the product.

Thinking of yourself as merchandise to be marketed to an employer may not seem flattering, but it's the most productive premise on which to base your job search. And, of course, you're not really selling yourself, but what you know and what you can do.

Your job-search sales campaign is a three-step process. You must first assess your skills and background and organize this information into an attractive, easy-to-read resume. Then you must sell yourself to an employer on the basis of the resume by writing an effective, targeted job application letter that gets you an interview. Finally, you must close the sale by taking an active role in the job interview.

Almost any book on the job-search process—and there are dozens on the market—will give you a list of rules to follow in accomplishing these three objectives. In fact, some books are so detailed and specific that they even tell you where to set the margins on your typewriter. These books seem to imply that there is only one "correct" way to write a resume or job application letter and that, if you follow the rules exactly, you are bound to be successful.

These formula books are very popular, and for good reason. They make the process of getting a job look easy. In fact, as you already know, getting a job is hard work. Even at this stage of your job-search sales campaign, you've probably found that the job market is complicated and that you have lots of competition for the job you want. Whatever your field of interest, chances are it is crowded with people just like you who want to put their education and experience to work in a challenging, high-paying job. To compete with them and win, you will have work harder at marketing your skills than they do at marketing theirs. This means that you will first have to research the job market thoroughly, then assess your qualifications to see how you can fit in.

Anyone can follow rules. Thinking about yourself and the job you want is the hard part. Yet, it's the thinking you put into your job search that will give you an edge in competing with other qualified applicants.

That's why this book is different from others you could study. Instead of telling you to follow the rules passively, *Getting a Job* asks you to take an active role in the job-search process—in effect, to teach yourself. Your goal is to develop your judgment about what is appropriate for the existing job market and for your particular situation, temperament, and background. To help you work toward this goal, the book presents you not with one correct and absolutely infallible model for writing resumes and job application letters, but with a number of examples to evaluate. Some of these examples are much better than others. Your job is to decide why.

Most books on the job-search process provide readers only with flawless models. But as you read through this book, you'll find several examples in which either the applicant's credentials are weak or the applicant presents his or her credentials in an ineffective manner. These negative examples are included for two reasons. First, there aren't any flawless human beings. Each person is *one of a kind,* someone with particular problems and goals. No one is *typical,* as a "perfect" model resume assumes. It is hoped that you will recognize some of your own circumstances in one or two of the models and that completing the informal exercises and assignments in this book will help you understand how best to package your own unique set of qualifications. Second, these negative examples are included because often analyzing why something is wrong helps in understanding what is right.

There is also a great deal of repetition in this book. Again, this is deliberate. Becoming skillful at the job-search process—like becoming skillful at the job itself once you are hired—is a matter of practice.

Of course, no book can guarantee you a job. But if you make the extra effort to think for yourself—and about yourself—and to analyze why some approaches to getting a job might be more effective than others, you'll be placing yourself one step ahead of the competition.

This text was improved by the helpful comments and suggestions of the following reviewers: Rita J. Bova, Columbus State Community College; Kin Norman, DeVry Institute of Technology—Kansas City; Al Past, Bee County College; William S. Pfeiffer, Southern College of Technology; Ned Putzell, DeVry Institute of Technology—Decatur, Georgia; and Jackie Zrubek, Texas State Technical Institute. I also extend my thanks to the editorial and production staff at Merrill Publishing Company; in particular, John Yarley, administrative editor, and Linda Bayma, production coordinator.

contents

part I   Getting started

1   Getting your purpose clear, 3

Competing for employment, 4
Taking charge, 4
Selling yourself, 4
The service attitude, 5
Examples that reflect the service attitude, 6
Rewriting to reflect the service attitude, 6
Your turn, 6
Questions for discussion, 7
Discussion of chapter exercises, 7

2   Researching the job market, 9

The college placement office, 9
Creating a system, 10
Researching companies, 13
What not to do, 17

3   Assessing your abilities, 19

Recording your work experience, 19
Recording your educational experience, 25
Recording additional experience, 27
Analyzing your goals, preferences, and abilities, 29
Writing the career statement essay, 33
Collecting supporting documents, 36

part II   The resume

4   Chronological and functional resumes, 41

Making your resume stand out, 41
Two types of resumes, 42

Advantages of chronological and functional resumes, 42
Examples of chronological and functional resumes, 42
Case studies, 47
Your turn, 47
Questions for discussion, 48
Discussion of chapter exercises, 48

5 Order, manner, and depth of presentation, 51

Order of presentation, 51
Reorganizing exercise, 53
Your turn, 55
Manner of presentation, 55
Depth of presentation, 57
Discussion of chapter exercises, 58

6 Resume checklist and models for analysis, 61

The resume checklist, 61
Details, 64
Your turn, 65
Questions for discussion, 68
Discussion of chapter exercises, 68

part III The job application letter

7 Letter format, 73

Stationery, 74
Six parts of the business letter, 74
Other elements of the business letter, 77
Forms of indentation, 80
Punctuation, 82
Your turn, 83
Questions for discussion, 83

8 The application letter as a sales letter, 85

Action as the purpose of business letters, 85
Persuasion, 86
Standard three-part business letter organization, 86
Model sales letter, 87
Review, 89
Applying sales letter organization to the job application letter, 89
Your turn, 91
Discussion of chapter exercises, 92

9 Handling problems and establishing a businesslike tone, 95

Tailoring the opening for unsolicited applications, 96
Tone, 96
Letters for discussion, 99
Anticipating reasons for rejection, 103
Recasting negative factors in positive language, 104
Your turn, 104
Discussion of chapter exercises, 107

part IV The job interview

10 Anticipating the interview, 113

The purpose of interviews, 113
Staying in control, 114
Talking about yourself, 115
Planning what to say, 116
Interview questions that ask you to evaluate yourself, 119
Anticipating other general question areas, 119
Inappropriate and trick questions, 120
The question of salary, 121
Rehearsing for the interview, 121
Preparing questions to ask, 122
Interview situations for discussion, 123
Discussion of chapter exercises, 124

11 Handling the interview, 127

What to take to the interview, 128
Image, 128
Appearance, 129
Details, 129
Attitude, 130
Strategies for demonstrating your personality, 130
Pointers, 131
Recovering a fumble, 132
Questions for discussion, 133

12 Following up, 135

The follow-up letter, 135
Turning down a job, 136
Being turned down, 138
Persistence, 138
Reassessing yourself and your job-search strategies, 140

Index, 141

part I Getting started

1 Getting your purpose clear

Employers don't hire the person who is most qualified for a job. They hire the person who has *persuaded* them that he or she is most qualified. Sometimes the applicant is one and the same person, both well qualified and able to demonstrate that fact to the employer. Sometimes, however, applicants are well qualified but can't get that message across. They just aren't assertive enough.

Take the hypothetical examples of John and James. John begins his application letter this way:

> Dear Sir:
> I was wondering if you might possibly have some openings in your store for someone like me with only a two-year junior college degree.

James writes:

> Dear Mr. Addison:
> With the thorough background in retailing I acquired at Case Junior College, I believe I have the ability and drive necessary to serve your store well as a sales management trainee.

John puts himself down by minimizing his education; his approach is wishy-washy and timid. He doesn't even know the name of the person to whom he is writing or the job he wants. James, on the other hand, is confident. He did a little research to find out the name of the person to whom he should write and the sort of entry-level position he might reasonably hope to secure. He is proud of his education, as he should be. And, perhaps most important, he indicates clearly that he *wants the job*. If you were the employer, which applicant would you interview?

The examples of John and James are extreme, but they illustrate a point. Job applicants have a natural—and quite sensible—tendency to want to show respect for the potential employer and not to present themselves as arrogant know-it-alls. Ironically, when applicants are too timid, too reluctant to brag about their achievements, they can appear not to care whether or not they get the job.

Competing for employment

Being qualified is not enough to secure a good job. You must persuade the employer that you are right for the position, using the same sort of approach that sales people use when they try to persuade a customer to buy a product. You sell your qualifications to a potential employer by putting yourself in the employer's place and anticipating the sort of person he or she needs to hire, then taking action to prove to the employer that you are that sort of person.

If you are a student, this active mode of thinking and behaving may be somewhat foreign to you. Teachers usually tell their students how to complete an assignment, for example; but no employer will tell you what to do to get a job.

In addition, every student who turns in an assignment gets a grade. School is, in this sense, *inclusive,* as are many social situations. Everyone participates; and everyone, to an extent, is rewarded. The job market, on the other hand, is *exclusive*—a win/lose situation. You either get the job or you don't, and good jobs are scarce.

What's worse, the employer is trying, in a way, to make you lose. Of course, it's nothing personal. But the employer's job is to reduce the number of applicants to one. That means he or she is looking for reasons to reject your application. The faster employers can reduce the number of applicants by rejecting them, the sooner their work is done.

Taking charge

It's because getting a job is a win/lose situation that you must take an active—even an assertive—role in the job-search process. Many people wait to be "discovered" by an interested teacher, employment counselor, or interviewer. They think it is somehow bad form to "show off" in order to gain attention. Most people are reluctant to brag about their abilities.

You can't wait passively for an employer to "find" you, however. You must take charge of the job-search process in order to win.

Selling yourself

Throughout this book, the job-search process will be described as a sales campaign; the job seeker is, by implication, the "product" to be sold. This way of thinking about the job search and job applicant is, of course, metaphorical. You don't really sell yourself when you get a job; you sell what you know and what you can do.

Still, there are definite similarities between selling a car or a television set and selling human ability and potential. In both cases, the seller must put the buyer first, anticipate his or her needs, and then persuade the buyer that the product meets those needs.

For some people, the idea of selling themselves has negative connotations. It means pretending to be what they are not, even compromising personal principles for the sake of money.

This book is certainly not suggesting that you do anything of the sort. Your principles and sense of yourself are part of what makes you valuable to an employer and, above all, to yourself. You don't have to transform yourself into an egotist in order to get a job. What you must do, however, is honestly evaluate yourself. What skills and knowledge do you have that an employer would be willing to pay money to use? What are your traits and aspirations, and what sort of employment situation will nurture them and help you grow? Being assertive does not mean being aggressive, and selling yourself does not mean selling out. It means, on the contrary, that you know who you are and that you value yourself.

The service attitude

Anyone in business — especially in sales — understands the necessity of a service attitude toward the customer. Of course, the customer is *not* always right in a strictly logical sense. Nor is the employer. But the customer must be satisfied for the sale to go through. His or her needs and desires must be anticipated and met by the seller, or there is no sale. The customer must be *persuaded* to buy.

To anticipate what the customer/boss wants in an employee, job applicants must put their own needs aside and try to think like the employer. Here are three excerpts from job application letters. Put yourself in the place of an employer and evaluate the approaches of the three people trying to sell their qualifications. Do they persuade the employer to "buy"?

1. Getting this job is especially important to me because I have been out of work for six months and have two small children to support.
2. Your company would be an ideal place for me to begin building my career.
3. I am particularly interested in your corporation because it has a London office, and I have always wanted to live and work in England.

The same thing is wrong with all of these approaches. Each statement ignores the needs of the employer and talks about what the applicant wants. Notice all the personal pronouns — "me," "my," "I." Not one writer indicates how he or she could *serve* the employer on the job.

Despite how we sometimes talk about the job-search process, no employer ever really *gives* you a job. Employers don't sit down and think about your problems or what you want. They're too busy thinking about themselves: *How can our company boost sales? What sort of manager can improve employee performance in our eastside office? What designs or concepts will put us ahead of the competition?* These are the sorts of problems employers think about. And they are what you should be thinking about, too.

Examples that reflect the service attitude

Now take a look at these approaches:

1. My background in repairing motorcycles and mopeds would be of significant value to your organization as it expands its automotive parts merchandising division to include motorcycle parts.

2. As the enclosed resume shows, I have a thorough background in computer programming. I also speak and write Spanish fluently, an ability that would allow me to deal effectively with your Spanish-speaking clients.

3. As you know, my father and brother are also journalists. Having grown up with an awareness of the problems and responsibilities of working reporters, I think I have an edge on other recent journalism graduates. I have no illusions about the long hours and hard work that will be required of me as a reporter on your paper.

These writers haven't groveled; they have merely put their own wishes aside and shown an awareness of the employer's needs: someone who speaks Spanish, someone who will work hard, someone who is aware of the company's expansion plans and sees how he or she can fit in.

Rewriting to reflect the service attitude

The service attitude does not mean that you behave like a servant. It means that you let two basic questions guide your approach to an employer: what kind of person does the employer need to fill this job, and what abilities can I offer that fit those needs?

Rewrite the following statements to reflect a service attitude:

1. I've had so many dead-end jobs in the past three years; I really want to find something I can stick with.

2. After four years as a poor college student, I'm anxious to put away my books and start earning a good salary.

3. My uncle is A. D. Peterson, the well-known banker. He says your company would be a great stepping-stone for me as I work my way up in the business. I'm willing to learn on the job.

After you have rewritten these three statements, turn to the end of the chapter for a discussion of ways to rewrite reflecting the service attitude.

Your turn

Now think about your own experience and imagine a job for which you are applying. In the following spaces, write three service-oriented statements about specific aspects of your qualifications and background that might convince an employer that you are the solution to a particular business problem. Don't invent fantastic credentials for yourself. Remember, sometimes an honest, direct statement of your intention to work hard is the most effective service-oriented statement you can make.

1. _____
   _____
   _____
   _____
   _____

2. _____
   _____
   _____
   _____
   _____

3. _____
   _____
   _____
   _____
   _____

Questions for discussion

1. Think about recent business experiences you have had. Can you cite both positive and negative examples of the service attitude? If you have recently encountered someone in business with a poor service attitude, what could that person have done or said to reflect a positive attitude?

2. If you have worked at a paying job, compare it to your school life or to volunteer work you have done. Are the skills and responses required of you on the job different from those required of you in volunteer positions or at school? Which environment is more comfortable for you and why?

Discussion of chapter exercises

Rewriting to reflect the service attitude, page 6:

1. Having had a number of menial jobs is not necessarily a drawback, especially if you are just beginning your career. So state your experience in a positive manner. For example:

> As you can see, I've had a number of jobs over
> the past three years. Each one has been a
> valuable learning experience for me, and I am
> confident now that I have the initiative and

> background to serve your company well in a number of capacities.

Or:

> As my resume shows, I've explored several career options. Each job taught me something, but the most important lesson I have learned in the past three years is that I do want to work in engineering. I am certain of my career goals now and am eager to put my experience to work for you.

In any discussion of your background, look for the positive aspects. Did you learn something, even something negative, about yourself from your work? Did you add to your list of skills? Did the variety of work you did make you resourceful, determined to succeed, adaptable? Did it teach you to get along with all sorts of people or work under less-than-ideal conditions? Think positive. What have you gained from your experience that would serve the needs of the employer?

2. It is assumed that you wish to be paid for your work and that you will be. Unless an employer specifically requests your salary history, never discuss salary in a job application letter or resume. Salary is a benefit to you, not to the employer. Further, don't try to sound eager for a job by minimizing what you did before. (Incidentally, the correct word here is "eager." "Anxious" means "*worried*." You may be anxious to get a job, but don't say so.)

The employer doesn't care whether you liked school or not, whether you were rich or poor. Don't be personal. Instead, try something like this:

> I enjoyed my college years, but I am eager now to put my education to work for you.

3. Don't try to impress an employer with your connections—or at least don't be as obvious about it as this writer was. And, of course, don't tell an employer you are just using his or her firm to get ahead. Talk about the job at hand. No one expects you to spend all your life at the same job, but there is no need to say you intend to move on after a year or two. Why reveal your plans to the employer before you even have the job?

It's okay to say that you know you can learn a lot from working at a particular job, but stress what you already have to offer as well. The remark that the writer is "willing" to learn might well strike the reader as ironically generous. Watch for unintentional arrogance in your choice of words. Suggested rewrite:

> Seneca University gave me excellent training in accounting principles; now I am eager to gain practical experience. I'm familiar with your firm's fine reputation in this community, and I know I would learn a great deal working for you.

2 Researching the job market

This book assumes you have decided on the kind of work you wish to do and that you have spent the past few years training for your career. Thus, you already have a good general idea of who's doing what in your field, what kinds of jobs are available, and what skills you need to get those jobs. Now you need to pin down your general knowledge to specific jobs and specific contacts. This means researching your field.

The college placement office

The first step in researching the job market is to visit the placement office of your school. Even if you are not currently enrolled, stop by. You will not be eligible to use all the office's services, and you may have to pay for some services students receive free, but the placement staff might let you browse through their information and read the company literature they keep on file. Placement offices usually offer services to the school's alumni and alumnae as well as to currently enrolled students, and many college and university placement offices provide career services to their communities. At the least, the staff will be able to direct you to government and private agencies that can help you. College placement personnel want to help.

College placement offices typically offer the following services:

- Helping students identify or clarify their career goals
- Helping students plan academic programs to achieve career goals
- Organizing on-campus student interviews with recruiters from major companies
- Maintaining libraries of reference books and information about specific companies

- Referring qualified students to local employers with positions to fill
- Maintaining lists of available on-campus and local job openings
- Inviting business and government representatives to visit the campus for a "career day" or "job fair" during which students can learn about various companies
- Offering instruction in career planning, resume writing, and interviewing

Of course, the services that placement offices provide vary from campus to campus. Among the most important functions are arranging on-campus interviews with company recruiters and keeping lists of current openings and files of information sent to them by major companies. Most placement offices are equipped to provide testing and counseling to help you decide exactly what sort of job is best for you.

You need not know exactly what you want from the office in order to begin an association with the people there, however. Just stop by and ask what services are available. The office staff will take it from there.

Keep asking questions; no question is too basic. Applying for a job is a skill. It can — and must — be learned. And the people in the placement office are experts at keeping current on the job market and teaching you the best strategies for securing a job. Be honest with the placement people. If you are confused about what you want to do, for example, let them know. They can help.

Creating a system

The placement office is your best ally in looking for employment, but the staff there can't do the looking for you. You have to take the initiative and develop your own job-search system. You'll need to build a network of contacts, collect and study information on the job market and specific companies, and organize a file system for your information and contacts.

Building a network of contacts

Every job seeker has access to a great number of contacts. He or she knows five to ten useful people, and these people, in turn, know five to ten more who, in their turn, know more people still. In other words, you are already part of a network of hundreds of people who might be able to help you find employment. The only problem is how to reach them.

The most obvious place to begin building a network of contacts is within your school. Your professors probably know people working in your field. **Make appointments with professors you know well** and ask them for advice. Do they know people you might contact or companies to which you might write? Talk with your professors, too, about their assessments of your strengths and weaknesses, your aptitudes, your abilities. Ask where they think you might fit in best. Try to get specific information — the names, addresses, and telephone numbers of other people you can contact.

The placement office — or perhaps the alumni office — of your school will have a list of alumni and alumnae. Check to see if anyone on the list is doing what you want to do. If so, get that name, address, and telephone number, too.

Next, **think about other people you know** who might be able to help you, people who work or teach in the field you wish to enter or know someone who does: friends, relatives, former employers, parents, church leaders. **Jot down the names on a tentative contact list.** The more you think, the more names will occur to you: parents of college friends, neighbors, sons and daughters of neighbors, alumni and alumnae of your school. Don't eliminate anyone at this point. Write down every possible contact, even those who seem unlikely.

Put the list aside temporarily while you begin working on other facets of your job search: collecting information on companies and drafting your resume. **When you return to the list, delete the names of people it might be inappropriate or useless to contact. Then divide the remaining names into three categories according to how helpful you think each person might be.**

Your professors will be in the first category, along with others who are excellent contacts (people in your field with hiring functions, perhaps relatives or close friends who work in your field). These will be the people you will contact first. The second category will contain the names of people who will *probably* be helpful, and the third category will contain the names of people who *might* be helpful.

You'll probably have about twenty or thirty names, with five to ten in each of the three categories. **Buy some 5″ × 7″ index cards and write the name, occupation, business address, and telephone number of each contact on a separate card.** Include any additional information that seems relevant. For example: "Knows president of Allied, Inc." Or: "Used to work for Hanson Manufacturing." Assign each card a category code letter (A, for example, for those people you intend to contact first) and sort the cards into three stacks: A, B, and C. **Alphabetize the cards in each stack by the contact's last name and store the cards in a file box.** As you contact each person, you will use these cards to record the date and results of the contact.

Study the sample index card on page 12. Notice that it provides a brief but complete record of the job seeker's relationship with Peterson, making it easy for the job seeker to follow up on Peterson's offer to help, for example. Notice, too, that the job seeker not only has kept Peterson informed of his or her activities, but has kept up on Peterson's career as well. The idea of establishing a network of contacts is not simply to use people once to get a job, but to develop a lasting professional relationship with a number of people in your field. Most workers have up to half a dozen different jobs during their careers. If you use your system to keep current on developments and personnel changes within your field, you will have the knowledge you need even after you are employed to move to a better position. In other words, a good system will allow you to remain within an active, profitable professional network.

Collecting information about companies

Now that you have a file of contacts, you will need to make a similar file for information on the companies in which you are interested. Follow the same general procedure: **make a tentative list of all the companies where you might work; then cut it down to just those companies for which you really want to work.** Let your preference be your guide here. Don't prejudge whether you *can* get a job with the company you want. That's for the

```
Peterson, John D.
Progressive Dynamics Corp.
44 Ryan Drive
Chicago, IL 60658
(312) 555-4599, ext. 471

Note: 23 years with PDC, influential in hiring



Contacted 4/21/1987, recommended additional course
   work in design, offered help in future
Contacted 9/18/1988, referral to Dean Mosley,
   head of design dept, Apac Corporation,
   Detroit, Mi. (see Mosley, Dean in file)
Peterson given Public Relations Dept in
   addition to Marketing, 11/13/1988
Contacted 7/20/1989, regarding opportunities at
   PDC, nothing available yet
Wrote follow-up letter, 11/29/1989, expressing
   continued interest
```

company to decide. Again, **divide your list into three categories: first choice, second choice, and third choice**.

In organizing your company files, **use file folders** rather than index cards. You will need to keep the company literature you collect and copies of the letters you write to and receive from each company. **You might also want a file for correspondence to and from your contacts and a file of job advertisements clipped from newspapers and professional journals to help you keep track of who is hiring and for what positions.** You might even want to cross-index people and companies or companies and salary ranges. The details of your filing system are up to you.

At first thought, making a file system for your job-search activities may seem like a fussy time-waster. After all, if you are a student, the placement office will probably be keeping most of the information you need on file. That office may even have a file on you, containing your transcripts and resume. Further, you may argue, you will be looking for work for only a short time and will probably contact only three or four companies.

It would be nice not to need a job-search file because that would mean that you would be hired by the first company you applied to for the ideal job, a job you liked so well that you kept it the rest of your life. But, of course, the job market doesn't work that way. As your job search progresses, you will probably find yourself exploring many more options and interviewing with many more companies than you thought you would. It's difficult to remember what was said at every interview. And paper accumulates surprisingly fast once you begin your active job search. You will need a system just for keeping the brochures, booklets, and letters you collect.

Your filing system will be more than a storage bin, however. It will be a way for you to learn about the job market you want to enter. More important, if you maintain your system well by making and filing notes after each contact and interview and by making copies of all the letters you write, it will be a convenient tool for retrieving the information you need.

For example, suppose you interview with Hadley & Smith early in April and nothing comes of the interview. In August, a representative from the company phones you; the person who was hired has not worked out, and Hadley & Smith is offering you a second interview. *If* you took notes after your first interview and kept them in your file system, along with the Hadley & Smith literature you collected and the correspondence you sent to or received from the firm, you are in a good position to interview quickly and effectively. If not, you'll have to do your research and preparation all over again.

Researching companies

If there is a secret to a successful job search, it is being prepared to take advantage of an opportunity when it appears. Some job-search experts would even say that being prepared and well organized can *make* opportunities appear. Job interviews set up for you by college placement offices are wonderful opportunities, but you might as well not bother to go to the interview if you are not prepared for it. To be prepared, you must know how to interview, a skill you will study later in this book. But being prepared also means that you must know a great deal about the company and about how you can fit into it. In other words, you must have done some research.

Again, your first stop as you begin to research is the college placement office. Companies routinely send placement offices company literature and notices of job openings. Most placement offices also maintain a library of helpful books and directories: Dun & Bradstreet directories and *Thomas' Register,* which list the product lines and locations of various businesses; directories of professional associations to which you might write; and *Standard and Poor's Register of Corporations, Directors and Executives.*

The next stop is the campus or city library. Look through the *Readers' Guide to Periodical Literature,* a reference that lists all the articles that have appeared in magazines and journals. Look first under the name of the company in which you are interested, then under the name of your field of interest (for example, "Engineering, electrical"). If you are interested in a particular facet of your field, try looking under other key indexing words, including product names or names of people in the field. Start with the most recent *Guide* and go back a year or two. When you find a relevant article, get it from the library and read it. And **take notes.** Here's a list of the kind of information you should look for:

- *History of the company.* Who started the firm and when? How has the company grown?
- *Product lines and services.* What *exactly* does the company make or do? What is its most successful product or venture?
- *Principals, locations, and affiliates.* Who are the company's leaders and why are they successful? Where are plants and offices located? With what other companies is the firm connected and in what way?
- *Current status.* How is the firm perceived by the public and by others in the field? Does the company face any problems (strong competition, heavy regulation)? Is it experiencing growth?

13

■ *Future plans.* Will the company be expanding, developing new products or services? What conditions or events could affect the company in the future?

While you are in the periodical section of the library, glance through the most recent issues of magazines and journals in your field. Take a look at the *Wall Street Journal, Forbes,* and *Fortune,* too. Skim to get a general sense of what's going on in business and industry, and try to get a sense of the style of corporations. This kind of study won't *make* you a corporate leader, but it may make you feel a little less like a student and a little more like a professional.

The research interview

Finally, **talk to people**. Call your contacts or write and request an interview. You won't be asking for a job, although the person with whom you talk might prove to be a potential employer. Instead, you will be asking for information. The research interview, one in which you seek information and guidance rather than a job, is excellent, low-pressure training for "real" interviews. It both teaches you how to interview effectively and gives you knowledge with which to impress employers.

Most professionals are asked often for advice, and most are glad to give it. But don't waste the person's time. Have specific questions prepared in advance. Here's a sample:

■ I want to go into research. What's the best way to prepare?

■ I'd like to stay in this part of the country. What sort of employment opportunities do you anticipate will exist here five years from now?

■ What sort of competition will I be up against when I begin interviewing? What's the best way to impress an interviewer?

■ What facets of the industry are growing? What's the best area to get into now?

■ With my background, where would I be most likely to fit in? What specific jobs am I most suited for?

If you have your resume prepared, take it with you, along with a copy of your transcript. Ask the person to evaluate your resume and make suggestions. Ask for an honest opinion of how your credentials stack up against those of other candidates. Ask the person about his or her own background. It's instructive to learn how successful people have structured their careers. Ask what you should do to sharpen your skills and add to your background.

Finally, and most important, ask for referrals to other people with whom you can talk. What you especially want to learn in research interviews is *whom* to talk with in order to get hired and precisely what job you should be aiming for. Sending out hundreds of resumes cold to company personnel departments is *not* the way to get an interview. Most corporate personnel departments are in the business of deflecting applications. You have to make contact with the person who has the power to hire you. Don't just ask who is president or personnel director of a company; ask also who is in charge of the department in which you want to work. Ask who makes the hiring decisions. This is the person with whom you may eventually interview and often the person to whom you should send your resume and application letter. When you leave the interview, put all you have learned into detailed notes as soon as possible and file them.

The company evaluation form

As you begin to learn more about the various companies in your field, organize the information on a simple form like the one on the next page. Completing a detailed evaluation form for each company you are interested in will help you to separate the pertinent information from the wealth of material you collect. The forms will also enable you to compare companies easily.

COMPANY EVALUATION FORM

Name of company: _____

Address: _____

_____

Telephone: _____

Nature of business: _____

_____

_____

Types of openings: _____

_____

_____

Requirements: _____

_____

_____

Hiring person: _____

Salary range: _____

Benefits: _____

_____

Promotion opportunities: _____

_____

Location of plants, outlets: _____

_____

_____

General remarks: _____

_____

_____

What not to do

Although it's admirable to leave no stone unturned in looking for work, some approaches are more productive than others. Knowing someone or, as discussed before, getting to know someone who can hire you is, obviously, the most efficient way to get a job. Other ways are less efficient.

The shotgun technique

The shotgun technique, discussed in passing earlier, consists of contacting large numbers of employers cold. Some job seekers sit down with a telephone and a phone book and call every firm in their field in an attempt to get interview appointments. If you have ever had someone try to sell you insurance or aluminum siding over the phone, you realize how pointless it probably is to use the telephone to contact employers. It's simply too easy for them to get rid of you.

A more common example of the shotgun technique is for a job seeker to have dozens or even hundreds of copies of his or her resume printed and then to mail them to corporate executives or personnel departments. These candidates reason that if enough copies of their resumes are circulating, sooner or later *somebody* is going to decide to interview them. This approach might just as well be called the "slot machine technique" because a job seeker's odds are about as good with this method as they would be if he or she dropped dozens of coins into a slot machine. The technique *might* pay off, but don't bet on it. Companies simply receive too many unsolicited resumes.

Applying from newspaper ads

You should be scanning the employment ads in the classified advertising section of your local newspaper and reading professional magazines for ads that appear there. This will give you a good idea of what job openings exist and what qualifications you need to be hired. But realize as you do so that not all professional-level positions are advertised.

Waiting for a good job to show up in the newspaper is a passive job-search technique. You may find a job that way, but it's easy to overlook a significant opportunity; and when a good job is advertised, you'll be applying cold, along with many other applicants with much the same kind of background you have. Many people have gotten good jobs through the newspaper, but don't count on the paper as your *only* source of information about the job market. Search actively. Your best route to a good job is through people you know or get to know by research interviewing.

Agencies

You may want to explore the option of using professional employment agencies to get a job. For a fee—paid either by you or the employer—these firms will attempt to match your qualifications to the needs of an employer who has contacted them. Before you pay an agency any money, however, find out exactly what it will do to help you get a job. Then ask yourself whether the agency can do anything for you that you can't do for yourself and whether it is likely to work as hard in your behalf as you yourself will.

State agencies do not charge a fee and might be worth investigating. But professional agencies are probably not a good bet. Most professional agencies are paid by the employer and receive a percentage of the employee's first month's or year's salary. It stands to reason, therefore, that an agency will be more interested in serving the employer than the employee and more interested in placing a highly paid executive than an entry-level candidate. It's appealing to think that someone else can and will do the work of finding a job for you, but in most cases, it just isn't true. Getting a job remains a do-it-yourself project.

3 Assessing your abilities

Salespeople have a cardinal rule: know your product. The same advice applies to job seekers. Assessing your skills, personality, and experience is an important step in the job-search process.

Some people know themselves very well. Others need to work at discovering and articulating their abilities and aspirations. The exercises that follow are designed to help you get to know yourself better and, even more important, to help you put what you know into words.

Before you can begin to design your resume, you'll need to collect and arrange the facts regarding your work history and educational background. What was your first job and when did you begin to work at it? What were your duties, your salary, your supervisor's name? You may think you can recite your life story easily, but specific details are sometimes difficult to recall. It's a good idea to have all the relevant information regarding your work and educational history collected, organized, and on file for reference. Chances are that you won't use all the information these exercises call for when designing your resume, but you may need it to complete a company application form.

Recording your work experience

Begin by recording your work history on the forms provided on the next several pages. Take time to fill them out as completely as possible. Begin with your most recent work experience and work backward to your first, using as many of the forms as necessary.

Take extra time to recall your duties in each job. List as many as possible and be specific. For example, don't just write: "Sales work in custom drapery department." Break down the work into specific tasks: "Advised customers regarding color and fabric selection, placed back orders, handled complaints, operated cash register." Then abstract from your duties the abilities you acquired in performing them and enter these abilities beside the heading "Abilities Acquired." In the example just cited, a worker may have strengthened his or her record-keeping skills, expertise in interior design, or ability to work with the public.

Has your work experience taught you to:

- Work well with people?
- Handle problems and complaints?
- Supervise others?
- Manage a petty cash fund?
- Lead others?
- Talk before large groups of people?
- Write well?
- Operate a word processor or other business machines and equipment?

Think, too, about any extra duties you might have performed. Did you ever fill in for other workers and carry out their duties? Did you act as someone's unofficial assistant? In most jobs, a worker will perform duties beyond the job description.

WORK EXPERIENCE RECORD

Name of firm: _____

Address: _____

Telephone: _____

Dates of employment: From _____ to _____

Job title: _____

Duties: _____

_____

_____

_____

_____

Abilities acquired: _____

_____

_____

_____

_____

Best part of the job: _____

Worst part of the job: _____

Name of supervisor: _____

Hours worked: _____

Rate of pay: Beginning _____ Final _____

Reason for leaving: _____

WORK EXPERIENCE RECORD

Name of firm: _____

Address: _____

Telephone: _____

Dates of employment: From _____ to _____

Job title: _____

Duties: _____

_____

_____

_____

_____

Abilities acquired: _____

_____

_____

_____

_____

Best part of the job: _____

Worst part of the job: _____

Name of supervisor: _____

Hours worked: _____

Rate of pay: Beginning _____ Final _____

Reason for leaving: _____

Recording additional educational experience

If you have received training in addition to your college education (graduate school, work-study programs, on-the-job training programs, business or vocational schools), record that experience on the next form. You may need to modify this form to suit your particular background. Describe the amount and type of instruction you received. For example: "Night school through Dayton Public School System, 8 hours of lectures and discussion regarding small-business advertising techniques and public relations." Then explain how this additional training applies to your career goals. Does it make you a candidate for a management position? Does it fill in gaps in your college education? Does it update your skills?

ADDITIONAL EDUCATIONAL EXPERIENCE RECORD

Name of school: _____

Location: _____

_____

Type of school: _____

Dates attended: From _____ to _____

Degree or certificate and date received: _____

Description of instruction received: _____

_____

_____

_____

_____

_____

_____

Application to career goals: _____

_____

_____

_____

_____

_____

_____

_____

_____

_____

_____

_____

Writing the career statement essay

Notice that some parts of the work and education inventory forms ask you to state preferences and evaluate the experience you have had. The self-analysis worksheet you completed also asks you to explore your preferences. Knowing yourself is a tremendous advantage in structuring your career. It helps you understand what sort of job you are best qualified for and, therefore, most likely to get; and it keeps you "on track" as you move from job to job. Sadly, people often waste years in jobs that don't suit them and in which they cannot succeed.

To help you learn more about yourself and clarify your career goals, you are asked here to write a 300-word essay explaining why you chose the field you did and what you hope to do with your training and abilities.

This essay is only a start. As you work through the job-search process, you will undoubtedly revise the essay often to make it more precisely reflect your work preferences, abilities, and goals. Then, too, your goals may change in time. The career statement essay is not a contract; it doesn't bind you to any particular course of action or attitude. But having a written statement of your goals will help you focus on what you are doing. It's an essential preparation for the job interview.

For now, don't worry about your writing style or whether or not you sound "impressive." Just get your ideas down. Try this organizational pattern:

- *Paragraph 1* — Why you chose the field you did.
- *Paragraph 2* — Abilities and ambitions you had before you completed your training and how that training changed, strengthened, or added to those ambitions and abilities.
- *Paragraph 3* — Description of the entry-level job you would like to get, why you are qualified for the job, and what you think you would learn from it.
- *Paragraph 4* — Description of your ultimate career goals. Where would you like to be and what would you like to be doing ten years from now?

CAREER STATEMENT ESSAY

_____

_____

_____

_____

_____

_____

_____

_____

_____

_____

_____

_____

_____

_____

_____

_____

_____

_____

_____

_____

_____

_____

_____

_____

_____

Collecting supporting documents

Having collected the facts about your work and educational history, completed the self-analysis worksheet, and written your career goals essay, you now have most of the information you will need to write your resume, including some vocabulary and self-awareness with which to describe yourself. Buy a file folder, label it "Employment," make copies of the forms and essays from this book, and file them in the folder. Having all the material you need collected in one file will make writing your resume easier. The file will also provide a complete, organized, and portable package of information to take with you on job interviews.

In addition to the material you have collected so far, you could add the following documentation to your file.

References

Your potential employer will probably want you to furnish references. References are simply the names of people the employer can contact to verify statements you make on your resume. Usually, references are former teachers or employers, business associates, clergy, bankers, friends — people who know you and can discuss your character and experience. Always provide the business addresses and telephone numbers of the references so that the employer can contact them easily.

Most employment counselors advise applicants not to include references on the resume. (You may not wish your present employer — whom you list as a reference — to know you are looking for a new job, or you may want to use different references for different employment situations.) Instead, prepare a list of references on a separate sheet of paper so that you can furnish them quickly when the employer requests them. Be sure to contact each reference to ask permission to use him or her as a reference *before* you make your list. Some may not be willing to give you a recommendation. File your list in your employment folder.

Transcripts

If you are a recent university or college graduate, you should ask your school registrar for several copies of your academic transcripts. You may not always judge it appropriate to submit your transcripts along with your application package, but — assuming your grades are good — transcripts can be a significant selling device for you, showing the potential employer what courses you took and the grades and honors you received. Obviously, if your grades are not impressive, don't send transcripts unless the employer requests them.

Photographs

Actors and actresses routinely submit photographs of themselves when they apply for jobs because their ability to do the job depends, in part, on how they look. Photographs are not usually required for other kinds of applications, however. In what circumstances might it be a good idea to send a photo with your application? Does including a photograph of yourself seem egotistical? Is that necessarily bad?

Work samples

Professional writers have photocopies made of their work to include as samples of their writing when they apply for jobs. Professional photographers and illustrators also usually have some sort of portfolio assembled which contains samples of their work. Although you probably won't be assembling an elaborate portfolio of your previous work, you may have some bit of evidence of your ability that could be included in your job application package or presented to the employer at the interview. Have you been favorably written up in a magazine, newspaper, or newsletter? Do you have a letter of reference that could be included? Have you had anything published or won any awards? Some recent graduates take copies of major school projects with them to interviews as evidence of their abilities and interests. Think over your school career or recent job experience. Is there any document that might profitably be included in your application package?

part II The resume

4 Chronological and functional resumes

There is no "perfect" resume, no one way to organize information about your work and educational history that guarantees success. In fact, a resume that works well for a friend or relative may be all wrong for you. People are unique, and their resumes should reflect that fact.

Although every resume is slightly different, each follows — or should follow — traditional business practice. The resume should be typed or printed on 8¹/₂" × 11" white bond paper and should be no more than two pages long. A one-page resume is best. The resume should contain all the information the potential employer needs to assess your background, but not so much information that important points are buried in detail. It should be concise, factual, neat, error-free, and easy to read. *And* it should be designed to sell your credentials in about twenty seconds because that may be all the time a busy personnel manager or executive gives to reading the resume you've spent days writing.

Making your resume stand out

Think of the billboards erected along major highways. Weeks of planning and design went into each one. Advertising executives worried over each word, each detail of color and design. Yet you'll probably give their work a mere three-second glance as you drive by. The message has to reach you — and fix itself in your memory — that fast. Otherwise, the billboard is not effective.

Your resume is the same sort of advertising device. You'll spend hours combing it for errors, retyping it so that it looks just right on the page. But employers won't notice that it is properly centered and error-free (although they'll certainly notice if it isn't). What employers look for as they sort through dozens of resumes is one that gets its message across fast, one that stands out from the rest.

Making your resume distinctive does *not* mean submitting it on lime green paper or recorded on video cassette or drawn in comic book format. Unless you're seeking a job in advertising or show business—and you're *very* sure that your unusual resume won't backfire—stay away from "creative" approaches. Business people are, for the most part, conservative. They are looking for people who know what standard business practice is, workers who will fit into the business team, not eccentrics who will challenge the rules.

You can make your resume distinctive in subtle ways, however, by manipulating the elements of the standard resume format so that the resume you design presents your qualifications in the most favorable light. Every resume is made up of basic blocks of information: education, work experience, personal data, objectives. Every resume uses words to get the message across, and every resume uses indentation, underlining, type placement, and capitalization to create an attractive format. It's *how* you assemble these elements and the words you choose that determine whether your resume is an effective selling tool.

Two types of resumes

There are basically two types of resumes. *Chronological* resumes (sometimes called descriptive resumes) list experience in a time sequence, beginning with the most recent experience and working backward. *Functional* resumes group experience into categories to document certain areas of ability, often without reference to when the experience was gained. In other words, you can either organize your qualifications according to a time sequence, recording, in effect, your life history, or you can present yourself as a person with certain well-defined capabilities, minimizing when those capabilities were acquired.

Advantages of chronological and functional resumes

In some professions, great emphasis is placed on how the potential employee has directed his or her career. A person with a continuous work history who has progressed up the ladder would want to use a chronological resume to demonstrate that he or she has worked hard to gain experience and is now ready to take on the job sought. In professions such as law, medicine, academics, and politics, making the right "career moves" is important.

On the other hand, a person who has not worked for some years or who has held a number of part-time positions or jobs not directly related to the job in question might want to write a functional resume, stressing his or her abilities rather than work record. There are cases, too, where a combination of the chronological and functional approaches works best.

Examples of chronological and functional resumes

Take a look at the resumes on the following pages. Smith and Jones have experimented with the resume form by organizing their credentials in both chronological and functional formats. Which resumes are chronological, and which are functional? Which format, chronological or functional, is more effective for Smith's qualifications? Which for Jones's? After you have studied the resumes, read the discussion of them at the end of the chapter.

WILLIAM R. SMITH

778 Wabash Road, Fort Wayne, IN 46805
(219) 555-9782

Date and Place of Birth: 3/18/67, Fort Wayne, IN
Marital Status: Single

WORK EXPERIENCE

Service Station
Attendant
: Jerry's Conoco, 1338 Hull Road, Ft. Wayne, IN. August, 1988 to present. Supervisor: Jerry Brown. Duties: Waited on customers, did some work as mechanic.

Disc Jockey
: KGLO, 281 Locust St., Ft. Wayne, IN. Part-time, July, 1987 to February, 1988. Supervisor: Brad Conley, Station Manager. Duties: Played top 40 records and read copy on the air, 10 p.m. to midnight shift, helped plan play list, wrote some advertising copy, did some promotional appearances.

Waiter
: The Oak Room, Hotel Van Meter, 910 First Ave., Ft. Wayne, IN. Part-time, May, 1986 to May, 1987. Supervisor: Charles Kirby. Duties: Served food, cleared tables.

Counter
Person
: McDonald's, 4547 E. Grady Road, Ft. Wayne, IN. February, 1985 to March, 1986. Supervisor: Marilyn Woods. Duties: Wait on customers.

EDUCATION

B.A.
: Rolliston College, South Bend, IN. June, 1988. Major: Economics. Grade point average: 3.4. Captain of debating team.

HOBBIES

Computers: have designed numerous programs to suit the needs of friends and family members. Music: collect records and play bass with a small, nonprofessional group

JEAN LOUISE JONES

Address: 4797 Mill Road, Minneapolis, MN 55455
Telephone: (612) 555-4772
Marital Status: Single
Health: Excellent
Date of Birth: June 19, 1961
Place of Birth: Sacramento, California

JOB OBJECTIVE: Executive Secretary to the Corporate President

SECRETARIAL SKILLS:	Take dictation at 90 wpm Type at 60 wpm Trained on IBM and Kaypro word processors
PERSONAL QUALITIES:	Well organized Able to work under pressure Tactful in handling people Punctual and reliable
WORK ACHIEVEMENTS IN PREVIOUS JOBS:	Managed office staff of five Planned itineraries for business trips of sales staff and potential clients Set up filing system for correspondence and press clippings
WORK HISTORY:	Mannville, International, Minneapolis, MN, 1987 to present. Secretary to Donald Witmer, Corporate Vice President of Sales. Dancorp, Inc., Minneapolis, MN, 1985 to 1987. General Secretary in Sales Division. Interstate Life and Casualty, Sacramento, CA, 1981 to 1983. Typist.
EDUCATION:	University of Iowa, B.A., June, 1985. Graduated with honors in English. American College of Business, two- year degree in secretarial curriculum, May, 1981.

WILLIAM R. SMITH

778 Wabash Road, Fort Wayne, IN 46805
(219) 555-9782

Date and Place of Birth: 3/18/67, Fort Wayne, IN
Marital Status: Single

VOCATIONAL GOAL: Sales Trainee Position with Stereo/Video Store

AREAS OF EXPERTISE: Highly knowledgeable regarding professional
quality and home use stereo sound equipment, sound mixers,
computers, radios, VCRs, and television equipment; capable of
computer programming in BASIC; capable of repairing stereo
equipment; trained musician; highly knowledgeable regarding
contemporary music.

SALES ABILITY: Experienced in radio sales and advertising;
trained and experienced in ad copy writing; articulate and
confident communicator; background in economics.

PERSONAL QUALITIES: People-oriented and outgoing, cooperative
and hardworking.

SUMMARY OF BACKGROUND: As a Disc Jockey with KGLO in Ft. Wayne,
I gained hands-on experience with sophisticated electronic sound
equipment as well as an understanding of how people relate to
music and what they expect in sound quality. I also received
training at KGLO in advertising and sales principles by writing
advertising copy and selling products on the air.

    I have extensive additional experience in public contact
positions where I learned to deal effectively with people.

EDUCATION: B.A. from Rolliston College, South Bend, IN. Major in
economics. Captain of debating team.

JEAN LOUISE JONES

4797 Mill Road
Minneapolis, MN 55455

Home phone: (612) 555-4772   Work phone: (612) 555-1219

WORK EXPERIENCE:

Secretary to Corporate Vice President

Mannville, International, Minneapolis, MN, 1987 to present.
Supervisor: Donald Witmer, Corporate Vice President of
Sales. Duties included managing an office staff of five
people, establishing an efficient filing system for
correspondence and newspaper advertising clippings,
planning promotional trips for sales staff and clients,
taking dictation (90 wpm), word processing, telephone work
and typing (60 wpm).

Secretary, Sales Division

Dancorp, Inc., Minneapolis, MN, 1985 to 1987. General
secretary working for several executives. General
secretarial duties.

Typist

Interstate Life and Casualty, Sacramento, CA, 1981 to
1983.

EDUCATION:

University of Iowa

B.A. in English with honors, June, 1985.

American College of Business

Two-year secretarial degree, May, 1981.

PERSONAL DATA:

Born June 19, 1961, in Sacramento, CA, single and in excellent
health. Hobbies include tennis, reading, and travel. Most
recently traveled to New Orleans, Louisiana, in 1988 for
Mardi Gras celebration.

Case studies   The following five paragraphs represent imaginary work histories for five different people. Read through each paragraph, decide whether a chronological or functional resume would probably better present the worker's qualifications, and explain why. After you have decided for yourself, read the discussion of these case studies at the end of the chapter.

1. Anne Carter-Bowman is thirty-eight years old. She worked as a medical secretary for several years until her daughter was born. She quit working to stay home with her baby, and although she did some volunteer work at a local hospital and acted as an unpaid campaign manager for a friend who ran for city council, she did not hold a full-time job for quite a few years. Now her child is grown up, and Anne wants to return to work full-time.

2. Joel Henry Wilson just graduated from law school. His father paid all his school expenses, and it was not necessary for Joel to work while in school. Joel has no work history, but he was an excellent student and participated in a number of impressive extracurricular activities.

3. Cynthia Willis began working as a sales clerk at Bloomfield's department store right after she graduated from high school instead of going on to college. She worked hard, and about a year later was made department manager of women's sportswear. She liked her work and took some night classes in retailing at a nearby junior college. Eventually, she was promoted to assistant buyer. Working with the head buyer, Cynthia learned how to spot coming fashion trends and how to assess the local market. Now the head buyer is retiring, and Cynthia wants the job.

4. John Avery was a meat cutter at the local packing house for sixteen years, but he lost his job when the plant closed six months ago. There isn't another packing house within commuting distance, and John is reluctant to relocate because his wife has a good job and his children are still in school. Although his work experience is confined to one kind of job, John has many hobbies: woodworking, gardening, and raising and training hunting dogs.

5. David Grant took time off after graduating from engineering school and toured Europe by bicycle with friends. When he got back six months later, he had trouble getting a job in his field because of economic conditions in his part of the country. At the time, Grant didn't want to leave his hometown to look for work, and so he took temporary jobs as a bartender, store clerk, and delivery-van driver. Finally, two years later, he got a good job with a prestigious firm and worked there for three years. Now he wants to relocate to a larger city and needs to write a resume to send to potential employers.

Your turn   Now think about your own background, using the work you did in Chapter 3 as a basis. Which pattern, chronological or functional, better fits your experience and why? Based on the Smith and Jones models you studied, draft a tentative resume for yourself in each pattern. (Use plain white typing paper, and refer back to the forms you completed in Chapter 3 to help you abstract your abilities for the functional resume.) Then trade your two resumes for two from a classmate and let him or her judge which is more impressive to an objective reader. You do the same with your classmate's resumes.

Questions for discussion

1. What is the basic difference between a chronological and a functional resume? What is minimized and what is maximized in each form?

2. In what ways might the two forms be combined?

3. What is the advantage of adding the Job Objective or Vocational Goal section to a resume? When would it not be advisable to include such a section?

Discussion of chapter exercises

Examples of chronological and functional resumes, pages 43-46

The resumes on pages 43 and 46 are chronological resumes; those on pages 44 and 45 are functional resumes. Since Jones's background is a little more solid than Smith's, either form would display Jones's qualifications well. But the chronological resume probably would be more effective, particularly in view of the job she is seeking. All of her experience is relevant to the job, and there are no gaps in her work history. In other words, she has nothing she might want to minimize, as Mr. Smith does. So, in addition to her good experience, she would want to show the logical progression of her work from typist to executive secretary by using a chronological format. Pointing out this progression will help her persuade the employer that she is ready to take on the next step in the progression—secretary to the corporate president.

Smith, on the other hand, although he has ability, does not have a background that displays quite as well as Jones's. There are gaps in his work history which will show up in a chronological format, and some unrelated and not-so-impressive jobs should be minimized. Smith would be smart to use a functional format and tailor his resume to a specific job (as on p. 45). He is well qualified for the job he is seeking, but not in the conventional way. That is, he has not sold stereo equipment before. Many people, like Smith, are qualified for jobs they have never done before. Getting the job is, in part, a matter of arranging credentials in a way that proves the applicant is qualified.

Case studies, page 47

1. Like Smith, Carter-Bowman has good experience with which to secure a job, but it must be presented in such a manner that the employer will see how it is relevant. Because Carter-Bowman has a long gap in her work history and some unpaid—although still valid—work experience, the functional resume format would probably present her qualifications in the best light.

2. Wilson has no work history, and a chronological format—which *is* a history—would just emphasize that fact. He should spotlight his abilities—

gained from his course work and extracurricular activities—in a functional resume format.

3. Willis *does* want to emphasize her work history because it proves she has worked hard to earn the opportunity at a top job. The dedication and hard work her work history demonstrates are among her best credentials for the job. She should definitely use a chronological format.

4. Avery is in a difficult position. All his work experience is in one job, and that job doesn't exist anymore in his part of the country. Under these circumstances, the chronological format would be useless to him in securing a job in a new field. Avery will have to abstract the qualities he demonstrated in his old job (diligence, punctuality, willingness to learn, and so forth) and apply them to a new situation. He will also have to bring in data from outside his work history—abilities he acquired pursuing his hobbies, for example. He should use a functional resume format.

5. Either format might work for Grant. On the one hand, he will want to minimize his irrelevant job experience and the six-month gap in his work history; and a functional format would handle the problem. On the other hand, it would be a shame if his impressive job with the prestigious firm got minimized in the process. What might work best is a combination of the two forms. Grant could organize the resume in chronological order to spotlight his one impressive credential, which he would describe in great detail, then group his unimpressive jobs under a heading such as "Other Work Experience." Remember, although you can't put false information on a resume, you don't have to give *all* the information about yourself. Nor do you have to treat all information equally. If some of your credentials are more relevant to the job than others, make the resume reflect that fact.

5 Order, manner, and depth of presentation

By now, you will have realized that there is more to writing a resume than simply throwing a few facts on the page. Writing a resume is work. It requires you not only to recall and organize all the facts of your employment and educational history, but to analyze these facts to determine the best way to present your qualifications to an employer.

All this work pays off, however, by training you to think critically about your qualifications and your image. In writing the resume, you learn to know yourself—your strengths and weaknesses. You learn how to present your qualifications in the best light, both in writing and in an interview. If you are tempted to duck the work of writing a resume by hiring a professional resume-writing service, don't. The work they do won't help you in an interview; it won't help you plan your career. And there's always the danger that a resume-writing service will misrepresent you. Only you know exactly the image you want to present. The self-evaluation and career planning that go into a resume are your responsibility.

Having worked through the self-assessment forms in Chapter 3, you should have all the relevant facts about yourself collected, and you should have a good idea of your goals and abilities. Now you need to organize these facts. You know from reading the previous chapter that you can arrange them chronologically or according to function, but within those two general organizational patterns, many more choices must be made. In this chapter, you will study effective resume formatting in more detail.

Order of presentation

Three factors must be considered in organizing your data within the resume: the *order* of presentation, the *manner* of presentation, and the *depth* of presentation. Manner and depth of presentation will be considered later in this chapter.

Having studied chronological and functional resumes, you already know something about order of presentation. Chronological resumes present data in a time sequence (chronology); functional resumes ignore chronology and group skills and experience into general categories.

Order of presentation in a resume is based on the general writing principle that whatever fact or idea is placed first automatically receives more attention from the reader, with secondary emphasis falling on the last fact or idea mentioned. A reader's attention tends to wander in the middle of a piece of writing, particularly if the reader is reading quickly.

Check out this principle with your own reading. Chances are, you read the first few pages of a book chapter fairly closely; then you begin to skim, picking up just the headings and the first and last sentences of each paragraph. Well-written paragraphs are usually constructed in such a way that the first sentence states the main idea of the paragraph. The sentences following offer evidence for the main idea or amplify it, and the last sentence sums up the paragraph and provides a transition to the next idea. Thus, as you skim, reading just the first and last sentences, you learn the main ideas and organization of the chapter, minus the details.

Newspaper articles are also written with this principle in mind. The most important information is placed at the beginning of the article because newspaper writers know that their reader—like yours—may not read everything they write. Magazine articles are written the same way, and so are well-written business letters. As you will see in Chapter 8, the first sentence of your job application letter is especially important.

If this principle is valid, then your resume should display your most important credential near the top, perhaps just after your name and personal data, so that the reader sees it first. This organization creates a positive first impression of your qualifications.

Because most people "work their way up" in life, the best work or educational credential is usually the most recent one. A person's college degree, for example, is both more impressive and more recent than the high school diploma. A recent job is probably more impressive than one held five years before. Because people have this tendency to get better as they go along, most people's credentials fit well into a reverse chronology resume like the ones you studied in the last chapter.

Some people, however, do not have neatly progressive work and educational histories. They may have dropped out of school or held a number of unimpressive jobs. This doesn't mean their experience is unmarketable; it means simply that the experience does not fit the usual pattern and that another pattern must be found.

Just as you don't look your best in a suit or dress that doesn't fit you, your credentials don't display well in a resume format that doesn't fit them. In Chapter 5, you studied ways to tailor a resume's order of presentation to suit a particular goal and background. Look at the Smith and Jones resumes again (pp. 43-46), this time skimming them quickly as an employer would. On Smith's functional resume, the first thing you notice is that he has a "goal" and "expertise," and that he is "highly knowledgeable." The final bit of information you get is that Smith was "captain of the debating team." Don't his credentials shine more in the functional format than in the chronological, where he is identified at the top of the page as a "service station attendant"?

On the other hand, Jones's functional resume doesn't flatter her credentials. The format spotlights her "secretarial skills," but thousands of people have secretarial skills. What Jones wants to say is that she has *exceptional* secretarial skills, and the chronological format allows her to do that by putting her impressive current job as secretary to the corporate vice president in the most noticeable position on the page.

Reorganizing exercise

The McCormick resume on the following page is not incorrect, but it could be more effectively organized. Using what you have learned about the order of presentation in resume writing, reorganize and rewrite the resume. To help yourself think through the rewrite, first answer the following questions:

1. What is McCormick's best credential? _____

   _____

2. What is the major flaw in the resume?_____

   _____

3. What could be cut from the resume?_____

   _____

When you have rewritten the resume, turn to the discussion of the rewrite found at the end of the chapter.

Gale Ruth McCormick

School Address   Home Address

Room C219   5554 Pauley Drive
Riley Hall   Houston, TX 77265
Crestmoor College
New Orleans, LA 70115

Telephone

(504) 555-9257   (713) 555-5441

Height: 5'7"
Weight: 122 lb.
Age: 22
Hobbies: Tennis, stamp collecting, camping
Social security number: 000-00-0000
Place of birth: Houston, TX
Date of birth: May 29, 1967
Marital status: Single

EDUCATION

Sam Houston High School, Houston, TX, June, 1985.

Crestmoor College, New Orleans, LA, June, 1989 (expected date
  of graduation).

WORK EXPERIENCE

Cafeteria Helper, Crestmoor College, Sept., 1985 to present.
    Supervisor: Mrs. Grace Anderson. Duties: Assisting cooks,
    clean-up work

File Clerk, Allied Security, Houston, TX, June, 1987 to Sept.,
    1987. Supervisor: John Porter. Duties: Filing, answering
    telephone.

Waitress, Carl's Cafe, Houston, TX, May, 1985 to Aug., 1985.
Supervisor: Carl Billings. Duties: Waiting on customers.

Senate Page, United States Senate, Washington, D.C., Sept.,
    1984 to April, 1985. Duties: Running errands, delivering
    messages

REFERENCES

John Porter, Records Department Manager, Allied Security,
    41 Bennet St., Houston, TX, 77265. (713) 555-9108

Grace Anderson, Cafeteria Manager, Crestmoor College,
    New Orleans, LA 70115. (504) 555-9008

Your turn	In the last chapter, you were asked to draft two resumes, one chronological and one functional. Now compare the two formats. Which displays your credentials more effectively? In which is your most impressive credential spotlighted in a prominent place on the page? Which looks better? Which would get more attention from a busy executive skimming dozens of resumes? Remember, the key to organizing an effective resume is to put your best credential first, but save an impressive or memorable detail for the bottom of the page, too.

Discard the weaker format and consider the other a working draft of your final resume. As you read through this chapter and the next, apply what you learn about effective resume writing to this draft.

Manner of presentation

The manner of presentation in your resume refers to the way you put down information. Do you use phrases or full sentences to describe your duties? Do you list the job title first or the company for which you worked? How should a resume be punctuated? Manner of presentation, like order of presentation, is a matter of what comes first; but it is also a matter of consistency, style, and typography.

Sequence

Look again at the McCormick resume. The writer has listed her work experience by noting the job title first, then the place she worked, then the dates, the supervisor's name, and, finally, her duties on the job. This is the standard sequence of information, but notice that it doesn't represent McCormick very well.

Let's suppose Allied Security is a large, impressive firm. The fact that McCormick worked there, whatever her job, allows her to "borrow" some of that prestige. She can also borrow the prestige of Crestmoor College and certainly that of the United States Senate. In this writer's case, then, it might be more effective to list the name of the company first, then the job title. Or, even better, since McCormick's job titles are not impressive, she could omit them and move up the duties section, like this:

> Allied Security. Worked in Records Department,
>   filing documents and answering the
>   telephone. June, 1987 to Sept., 1987.
>   Supervisor: John Porter.

Recasting the elements of a job description, as in this example, won't totally change the nature of the job; McCormick was still a file clerk, not vice president. But it can help present the job in a better light. The idea is not to be pretentious—making a garbage collector into a "sanitation engineer," for example—but to give the work the description it deserves. And, after all, applicants are not titles, but *people* who perform specific duties on the job.

Consistency

So, as with the order of presentation, there is a usual manner of presenting information (job title, company, dates, supervisor, duties), and there are reasons to deviate from the usual way. No resume is exactly like any other, but every resume should be consistent in itself.

Consistency means that the resume writer follows, in every instance, the rules he or she has established for the resume. Thus, if McCormick has decided to list the company name first for the Allied Security entry, she must follow the same rule with Carl's Cafe.

Consistency also means that the writer must scrutinize punctuation, abbreviations, and other details of style. McCormick, for example, uses abbreviations for states in the top half of her resume; she cannot, then, switch to spelling out the name of the state in the Work Experience section. She has separated the elements of her first job description with commas, so she cannot switch to semicolons in the second entry. If she uses all capitals for "EDUCATION," she must use the same style for "WORK EXPERIENCE."

Look at the McCormick resume again, and note these inconsistencies: she fails to list a supervisor's name for her Senate page job; she omits final punctuation at the end of two of her job entries. Notice, too, that she uses a gerund (a verb ending in "-ing" and functioning as a noun) to describe all of her duties except one: clean-up work. Parallel ideas should be expressed in parallel form; that is, all the duties should be expressed as gerunds or they should all be expressed as nouns or verbs. For example: "Duties: clean-up work, message delivery, telephone work." Or: "Duties: answered telephone, ran errands, delivered messages, filed correspondence."

These details are easy to miss. Check the working draft of your resume. Is it consistent?

Writing style

Even though resumes are abbreviated "charts" of information rather than essays, they have a prose style. Skillful prose writers avoid abstract, vague nouns and weak verbs such as "to be" and "to do." They use, instead, precise nouns and active verbs, and they give enough specific detail to describe the job fully.

For example, instead of writing "Did accounting work," a precise writer would describe a job's duties this way: "Reconciled bank statements; posted business transactions, including allotments, disbursements, payroll deductions, and expense vouchers." Notice that this description not only gives a better idea of exactly what the applicant did on the job, but it also conveys a sense of the applicant's pride and expertise. The vague and lackluster phrase "did accounting work" suggests that the applicant wasn't interested in the work and can't remember much about it.

To inject a sense of action into your job descriptions, consider using precise, active verb forms such as these: "evaluated," "developed," "analyzed," "processed," "devised," "created," "performed," "formulated," "oversaw," "diagnosed," "promoted," "recorded," "assembled." Try to make your resume prose as precise as possible.

Typography

Typography refers to how print looks on the page. At first thought, it may seem as though the appearance of the resume is the least of an applicant's worries. After all, it's what the resume *says*, not how it looks, that will get the applicant an interview.

Yes and no. Employers don't expect—or even want—elaborate and expensively printed resumes. But how your resume looks does say something about you. If it's crowded and cluttered-looking, the employer may assume that you are disorganized. If there is too much "white space," the employer might get the impression that you are insufficiently qualified.

Resumes that don't look impressive and easy to read don't get read. Look again at McCormick's resume and compare it to the Smith and Jones resumes from Chapter 4. Apart from the information they contain, which resume looks best to you? If you were an employer, which resume would you read first, and why?

Depth of presentation

Experts on the job-search process often warn applicants not to make their resumes too long. A one-page or, at most, two-page resume is best. Ironically, the problem with most job applicants, particularly those who are just beginning their careers, is not that they say too much, but that they don't say nearly enough. Most people are reluctant to talk about themselves, and this tendency shows up on their resumes. Further, most people are not aware of just what they have to offer a potential employer. They don't know how to "read" their own background and often ignore or give insufficient attention to impressive credentials. In other words, they do not write their resume with enough depth of presentation.

Giving enough detail

Because their own experience is familiar, most people tend to underrate it. They forget or minimize facts about themselves that would impress someone else. That's why it's important, as you work on your resume, to spend enough time remembering the work and educational experiences you have had. Look over the work history forms you completed in Chapter 3 and see if you can add other duties you performed on each job. Did you supervise other people, handle cash, do any writing, make suggestions that were incorporated into the workplace, operate equipment, train other people, volunteer for extra duties? If so, be specific. These tasks, although they may not be directly related to your skills and training, show that you have initiative and that your boss trusted you to be responsible. If these good work-related traits paid off — if you were promoted to a better position with the same company or earned a raise in pay while on the job, for example — put that down, too.

Scrutinize your educational history in the same way. Did you do any special projects while in school, conduct any independent studies? Did you participate in an internship or co-op program? Did you earn any scholarships or awards? Put down every extracurricular activity.

You may be tempted to omit details of your background that you think would not interest an employer. Put them down anyway. Then show your work and educational histories to a classmate or two. Ask them what is particularly interesting or memorable about your background. Chances are, it will be something specific, something unique. Of course, you are not going to put everything you ever did on the resume, but you should have all the details about yourself on paper so that you know exactly what you have to choose from.

Including nonwork experience

People who are just beginning their careers sometimes say that they have no experience, no credentials other than their education to prove that they would be good workers. Of course, these people don't really mean that they have *no* experience. They mean that they have no experience at a paying job. Everyone has done something in his or her life other than attend school, and that activity says something about that person.

Prior work experience is, of course, an excellent credential, but it's not the only proof of your potential value that an employer will accept. Employers often need "raw recruits," people with potential whom the company can train. If you have not worked before, your challenge is to find ways to market the experience you *have* had, ways to turn elements of your background into evidence that will demonstrate your potential.

When employers hire at this level, they look not so much for experience as for work-related character traits: intelligence, initiative, organizational skills, a sense of responsibility. Anything you have done that demonstrates some positive trait should be mentioned: teaching Sunday school, earning the rank of Eagle Scout, customizing your car, working as a volunteer for a political candidate or a charitable organization. No matter how trivial or unrelated to the job an activity might seem, it taught you something and demonstrates something about you as a potential employee. Your task is to analyze the activity and bring out its meaning for the employer.

Discussion of chapter exercises

Reorganizing exercise, page 53

McCormick's best credential is probably her work as a Senate page. It's unusual and memorable, something about which she and an interviewer could converse. Not every applicant will have had this experience. But McCormick doesn't give it the prominence it deserves. That is a major flaw in the writing. Another—and even greater—flaw is that the top half of the resume is filled with routine information (addresses, telephone numbers, and so on) and unnecessary information that creates a boring first impression. By the time readers get to the important information, they will have probably lost interest.

The typography of McCormick's resume isn't great either, primarily because she has too much white space at the top of the page, too much print at the bottom. There are ways to tighten up the amount of space the routine information requires. For example, the reader can figure out which is McCormick's home address and which is her school address; these don't need to be identified. Likewise, most readers can recognize a set of numbers as a telephone number without it being so labeled. Cutting these labels saves two lines plus spacing lines.

McCormick also could cut a lot of unnecessary information such as her height and weight. Marital status is usually not important unless the applicant has dependents, so that line could be cut as well. McCormick's hobbies do not mark her as memorable and could be omitted with no loss. She gives both her age and her date of birth, a duplication that wastes space and marks her as thoughtless. Date of birth is preferred over age because the birth date will not change, whereas the age will.

Finally, McCormick doesn't give enough detail about the work she has done. She could cut the entry regarding her high school education since most employers will be interested only in college or trade school training.

With the extra space, she could expand on her college education. What courses did she study; what grades did she earn? Since her work experience is slight, this expanded Education section and an added Goals or Vocational Objective section would help make her resume more memorable.

A suggested reorganization of McCormick's credentials into a functional resume format appears on the following page. This rewrite, like your own, represents only one way of organizing the information. If your rewrite is different, that doesn't mean it is wrong.

GALE RUTH McCORMICK

Room C219   5554 Pauley Drive
Riley Hall   Houston, TX 77265
Crestmoor College   (713) 555-5441
New Orleans, LA 70115
(504) 555-9257

CAREER GOAL

As an honors graduate of Crestmoor College, I am
seeking a challenging career in retailing where I can
use my business training and my ability to work with
people.

WORK-RELATED QUALITIES

Responsibility: As a Senate Page in the United States Senate
                  in Washington, D.C. (Sept., 1984 to April,
                  1985), I delivered important messages within
                  the Senate chambers and between offices.

Accuracy: As a File Clerk at Allied Security in Houston,
                  TX (June, 1987 to Sept., 1987), I handled
                  company correspondence and insurance
                  policies quickly and accurately.

Initiative and   As a high school student, I worked as a waitress
Determination   to earn tuition for my first year of
                  college. Since I have been in college, I
                  have worked in the college cafeteria to help
                  support myself.

EDUCATION

Crestmoor College, New Orleans, LA, June, 1989 (expected date
    of graduation). Relevant courses: Retailing, Business
    English, Marketing, Accounting, and Economics. Major: English.
    Grade Point Avg.: 3.2

PERSONAL DATA

Date and Place of Birth: May 29, 1967, Houston, TX
Social Security Number: 000-00-0000
Hobbies: Collecting stamps from African countries, tent
         camping, tennis

6 Resume checklist and models for analysis

The resume—also sometimes called a personal data sheet or vita—is a chart of your professional life. An employer should be able to look at it and quickly gain both a general sense of your work and educational background and a specific idea as to how you are uniquely suited for the job to be filled.

Like any chart, the resume should be complete. If you use a chronological format, there should be no gaps in your work/educational history, no lengthy time period in your adult life not represented by an entry. In other words, the employer should be able to trace your professional history. If you use the functional format, the employer should still be able to determine quickly where you worked or went to school and when. Even though the functional resume minimizes chronology, it should nevertheless be specific, full of concrete details, including dates. Otherwise, the resume will seem vague and evasive.

Having explored and analyzed your background thoroughly and studied effective resume writing, you should have a good idea of how you want to present your qualifications to an employer through your resume. All that is left for you to do is polish your writing and check the details.

The resume checklist

The pointers on the next few pages review the details of resume writing. They represent standard practice, that is, the way most business people believe resumes should be designed and written. As you probably realize, the principles of order, manner, and depth of presentation which you studied in the previous chapter are inseparable. In practice, each element works with the others to create an effective resume. To help you think about your resume in a logical fashion, however, the pointers given here have been divided into the same three categories of presentation.

Work through the items in each category and think about why each particular "rule" was probably formulated. Then bring your resume draft into line with the advice this checklist offers. Later, you will be asked to polish a sample resume on the basis of what you have learned. Remember, it isn't necessarily "wrong" to deviate from the advice offered in this book, but have a good reason for doing so.

Order of presentation

1. Use your name—not "Resume"—as the heading, along with your address and telephone number. Your name should be typed in capital letters; your address and telephone number should take up a minimum amount of space.
2. If a Goals or Career Objective section is included, place it at the top, right after the heading.
3. Your best credential should appear in a prominent place so that it will be the first thing an employer notices while skimming your resume.
4. In a chronological resume format, use reverse chronology; that is, begin with your most recent experience and work backward in time.
5. If the job calls for an experienced worker, put your work experience before your educational experience. If the employer seems more interested in the educational background of applicants or you have little work experience, put your education first.
6. The Personal Data section generally contains some or all of the following: social security number, date and place of birth, marital status and number of dependents, military status if relevant, height, weight, health, membership in relevant organizations, licenses held if applicable, and hobbies. Include only what is relevant and impressive. This section can appear just after the heading or at the bottom of the page.
7. If references are listed, they should appear at the very bottom of the page.

Manner of presentation

1. The standard sequence of information within each job experience entry is: job title, name of company, address of company (or city and state), part-time designation if applicable (jobs are assumed to be permanent and full-time unless otherwise specified), dates worked, supervisor's name (optional), and duties. Information regarding salary and the reason for leaving is optional. Don't clutter up the resume with too much data. Include just what is essential or items that reflect well on you.
2. The usual sequence of information within each educational experience entry is: degree, school, location of school (city and state), date graduated, course of study, thesis and supervisor if relevant, grade point average (optional), and honors received if any. If the applicant has only one degree and wishes to emphasize the name of the school rather than the degree earned, he or she

can list the school first, then the degree, then the graduation date, and so on.

3. Information in an entry is ordinarily separated by commas. Some writers use a period following the dates, then periods and colons between remaining items. The item "Duties" is usually followed by a colon. Then the duties are listed, separated by commas. The complete entry should be followed by a period. For example:

Elementary School Teacher, General George Custer
    Elementary School, Oak Park, IL, Jan., 1988, to June, 1989.
    Principal: Miles Smythe. Duties: Teaching 120 third-grade
    students, supervising playground and cafeteria, tutoring
    Spanish-speaking students in reading, serving on library selection
    panel.

The purpose of punctuation is to clarify the entry. Any logical punctuation style is acceptable so long as the writer uses it consistently.

4. In listing duties or other information in the work and educational entries, noun or verb phrases are preferable to full sentences. Example: "Audited books monthly" or "Monthly auditing of books." Not: "I audited the books on a monthly basis." Avoid using personal pronouns ("I," "me," "my").

5. Emphasis can be achieved by underlining or capitalizing important words such as job titles or degrees earned. You may also want to use "hanging indention," in which every line of an entry is indented except the first. This form of indenting makes the first item in the entry stand out (see the example in item 3).

6. Resumes are fact sheets; opinions and persuasive language should be saved for the application letter.

7. Arrange elements on the page so that they make a pleasant "picture" of your qualifications. Cut the resume if it seems too cluttered and hard to read; add information if there is too much white space. Use headings to make categories of information easy to spot.

Depth of presentation

1. Describe work and educational experience in detail. Break down any job you have done into its components and list the components separately. Don't assume the employer knows what a job entails.

2. If you are short on experience, list relevant courses taken in school and describe them. Don't explain the obvious; but again, don't assume the employer knows the content of every college course. Note especially any lab work, field work, independent study, or special projects.

3. If you choose to list hobbies and extracurricular activities, make sure they display well; that is, choose items that are specific and memorable. Avoid general or vague entries such as "enjoy reading." Write instead what kind of reading you enjoy.

4. Don't put in headings for which there is little or no information. For example: "Publications: none." Likewise, don't make headings for information that puts conditions on your employment. For example: "Willing to travel" or "Unwilling to relocate."

5. Try not to leave gaps in your work/educational history. Employers want to be able to trace your professional history and may get suspicious if the resume seems vague and evasive.

   Even if you are using a functional format, it's a good idea to include a section at the bottom labeled "Work History" or "Past Employment" where you list jobs in reverse chronological order. Most employers expect to see work experience listed this way, and you should probably try to satisfy that expectation even if your work history is not impressive. But put the history at the bottom of the page. By the time the employer gets to this section, you will have had time to impress him or her with the top half of the resume.

6. Don't include so much information that the resume becomes cluttered or runs to three or four pages. A tight, well-organized one-page resume is almost always best. Be selective in what you include, and remember that you can group information under a catchall heading such as "Additional Experience" or "Part-time Work Experience." Use such a category to list items too insignificant to rate a separate entry.

7. If you elect to list references, make sure each person's job title, business address, and business telephone number are also listed so that the employer can contact the reference easily. It's a good idea, too, to note your relationship to the reference. For example: former employer, college advisor.

Details

Neatness counts in writing a resume. The resume can have *no* typographical or spelling errors. Proofread the copy carefully; then ask someone else to proof it. If you are not sure of your grammar or usage, have a more skillful writer look over your resume. This is not cheating; it's just common sense to recognize when you need help and to take action to get it.

The resume should not be bound in a binder or fancy folder; these are just a nuisance for employers who, you hope, will want to keep your resume on file. Nor do you need to include a picture of yourself with your resume.

As you continue to study resume writing and talk with counselors, teachers, and others, you will notice that ideas about the job-search process are often expressed as rules. Here are some common "rules" about writing and submitting resumes. Some are contradictory, so you can't agree with all of them. Which rules seem sensible to you? Do some rules make sense in one context but not in another?

1. Don't include information about the salary on your present or previous job; don't include your salary expectations for the job for which you are applying.

2. Don't forget to include ZIP codes and area codes for all addresses and telephone numbers. You may want to send your resume to another state or country.

3. Don't include personal physical details (height and weight, health problems, sex).

4. Don't include your references. The employer will need them only if he or she decides to make you an offer.

5. Always include your references. It's convenient for the employer and reflects a good service attitude.

6. Don't include your age. Some employers are biased against very young or very old applicants. Including your age on the resume gives employers too good an opportunity to reject you.

7. Do include your age. The employer needs to know this in order to evaluate your qualifications and because it affects the benefits you will be paid if you are employed.

8. Don't put down your marital status. It's not important.

9. Don't write: "References furnished upon request." It goes without saying that you will provide references if asked to do so.

10. Include only the years you worked at a job (1988 to 1989), not the month and year (June, 1988 to Jan., 1989).

11. Use your date of birth, not your age in years.

12. Include your social security number as a convenience to the employer.

Your turn

There are dozens of rules for the job-search process; but, as you are probably beginning to see, no set of rules can cover every possible resume situation. You have to use your *informed* judgment to decide what to include and what to omit, what to minimize and what to emphasize.

The resumes on the following pages represent two recent graduates in electrical engineering. These men have roughly the same background and qualifications. Yet one resume displays those qualifications much better than the other. Analyze the resumes. You should be able to see immediately which one is more effective, but can you tell why? First, write a short explanation of why the better resume *is* better. The numbers at the right side of each resume will help you identify specific parts that work for or against the applicant. Then, on a separate sheet of paper, rewrite the less effective resume, inventing whatever details about the applicant's background you may need. When you have finished your analysis and rewrite, turn to the end of the chapter for a discussion of the two resumes.

QUALIFACATIONS OF GEORGE REDMOND   1.

FOR WORK AS AN ELECTRICAL ENGINEER

Address: 3360 Harwood Ave.
         Newark, NJ
         07107
                                                    2.

Telephone: (201) 555-8765

Social Security Number: 000-00-0000
                                                    3.

Hobbies: Golf, reading

Height and Weight: 5'9", 160 lbs.   4.

Age: 26   5.

Education: B.S. in Electrical Engineering from Colby
Technical Institute, Paterson, NJ, 1985
                                                    6.

Work: Engineering apprentice for National Electronics,
Inc., Newark, NJ, 1987 to 1989.
      Electrical draftsman, Hollings/Graley, Newark, NJ,
May, 1986 to Aug., 1987, drafting work
      Security maintenance man, Creely's Department
Store, Newark, NJ, 1986   7.

References: George Redmond, Sr.   8.
            3360 Harwood Ave.

            Rev. Gerald Appley   9.
            Grace Lutheran Church
            Fifth and High Street
            Newark, NJ

            Buzz McGraw
            Supervisor
            Drafting Department
            Hollings/Graley
            Newark, NJ
                                                    10.

ROBERT J. STACEY

1420 Adler Road, Springfield, MA 01103   1.
(413) 555-8797

CAREER OBJECTIVE: 2.

To secure an entry-level position in research and
development with an electrical engineering firm

EDUCATIONAL BACKGROUND: 3.

B.S., Electrical Engineering, University of
    Massachusetts, Amherst, MA, June, 1989.
    Courses included extensive work in electrical   4.
    design and drafting. Senior report:
    "Safety and Security Factors in Electrical
    Design for Public Swimming Pools."

WORK HISTORY:

Electrical Design Assistant, Bryce Electric, Inc.,
    Boston, MA, part-time, June, 1988, to Sept., 1988.
    Supervisor: J. D. Patrick. Duties: participated
    in designing electrical components for industrial
    security systems; consulted with clients; directed
    testing operations to assure conformance with
    specifications.   5.

Electrician's Assistant, Russi Brothers, Electrical
    Contractors, Springfield, MA, summers of 1987 and
    1986. Supervisor: John Russi. Duties: Wiring
    private homes and commercial buildings; inspecting
    new and existing buildings for conformance with
    city building code; conferring with clients and
    estimating costs.   6.

Additional Experience includes work as a hardware store
sales clerk; work on a sodding crew; and work in a fast-
food restaurant.

PERSONAL DATA: 7.

Date and Place of Birth: Jan. 12, 1968, Springfield, MA   8.

Social Security Number: 000-00-0000   9.

Leisure Activities: Reading biography and sea adventure
    nonfiction, hiking, and swimming
                                                          10.

Questions for discussion

1. Experts on resume writing usually advise against using full sentences and personal pronouns such as "I" or "me," yet the McCormick resume rewrite at the end of Chapter 5 uses them. Do you think this writing style personalizes the resume or does it seem too pushy and bragging?

2. You've been given a lot of rules to follow in this chapter and the last. How important do you think it is to follow the rules? Do you think employers notice the details of format and style in a resume, or are they concerned only with an applicant's actual qualifications?

3. Look again at the functional resumes of Smith and Jones that you studied in Chapter 4 (pp. 44 and 45), and notice that whereas Jones includes a Work History section, Smith omits this element. Granted that Smith's work history is not as impressive as Jones's, is it honest nevertheless for Smith to leave out this information? How would an employer react to the omission? Does it make the resume seem as though Smith is hiding something?

Discussion of chapter exercises

Model resumes, pages 66 and 67

Stacey's resume is, of course, the more effective of the two. The poorly planned typography of Redmond's and the misspelled word in the heading would probably disqualify the applicant immediately in a competitive job market. After all, an employer might reason, an applicant who can't spell "qualifications" probably doesn't have any.

Here's a breakdown of the additional flaws in Redmond's resume (keyed by number):

1. This heading does specify the kind of work Redmond is seeking, but the misspelled word makes a negative first impression and the applicant's name does not stand out from the rest of the text.

2. The address here takes up too much space in relation to its importance.

3. Too much important space is wasted at the beginning of Redmond's resume with information that is unnecessary or unimpressive. Redmond's hobbies are not memorable, and they are certainly not the first thing the employer will want to know about him.

4. Height and weight are not important considerations for most jobs; this information should be omitted.

5. The applicant should include the date (and place) of his birth, not his age in years.

6. Redmond needs to use capitalization, underlining, and hanging indention to separate the information he lists under "Education" and "Work" and make it more inviting to read.

7. Redmond should have listed the duties he performed on each job; otherwise, the impression given is that the jobs were not significant and Redmond wasn't very interested in them.

8. Redmond's father is not an appropriate reference, and Redmond has not given a complete address. Also, Redmond has neglected to list ZIP codes and, more important, telephone numbers for his references.

9. It's generally not appropriate to use nicknames such as "Buzz" in formal business communication.

10. Redmond's resume is not attractively centered on the page. Too much white space appears at the bottom, creating the impression that Redmond ran out of things to say about himself; and most of the information appears on the left, giving the page an unbalanced appearance.

In comparison, here are the positive aspects of Stacey's resume (again keyed by number):

1. Stacey's heading is the kind most resume writers use: the applicant's name in capital letters and the address as one centered line, the telephone number as another. This format is neat and takes up minimum space.

2. Redmond's heading says he is applying for work as an electrical engineer, but Stacey's Career Objective section pinpoints more precisely the type of work Stacey is seeking. It's important in approaching an employer to know and express what you want from him or her. Too many applicants seem to be asking, "What have you got?" This failure to be specific about the kind of work sought shifts the responsibility for the applicant's career unfairly onto the employer.

3. Notice that Stacey's use of capitalization, underlining, and hanging indention creates an attractive and easy-to-read format.

4. Stacey lists evidence from his school career to prove he can do the job he specifies in his Career Objective section. He also lists a specific project he completed in school. These details show he took an interest in his work. Listing specific details also provides topics for discussion at the interview.

5. Stacey lists duties he performed while working. This gives the employer a much better sense of his qualifications than the job title alone provides and also shows his enthusiasm for the work.

6. Stacey has grouped less relevant experience under a general category. Although his work on the sodding crew or at the fast-food restaurant doesn't prove he's a good engineer, it does show he is willing to work and has probably developed some good work habits.

7. Putting the Personal Data section at the end of the resume rather than at the beginning probably makes more sense in most cases because this information becomes relevant only after the applicant has shown he or she is suited for the job.

8. Stacey includes both the date and place of his birth.

9. In listing nonwork interests, Stacey again has been specific; what he reads is certainly more memorable than the mere fact that he does read.

10. Stacey's resume fills the page attractively with neither too much nor too little information.

part III The job application letter

7 Letter format

The ability to write a correct and persuasive letter is one of the most useful skills a business person can develop. For the established worker, a good letter can secure an appointment with a client, a healthy sales order, or a promotion; and for the person looking for work, it can persuade an employer to grant that all-important interview.

Of course, the most persuasive part of a business letter is the *content*—what the letter says and the way it says it. You will be studying content in chapters 8 and 9 of this book. This chapter deals with *format*, that is, the way the letter looks on the page. Although there are various approaches to the content of a letter, the letter's format is largely a matter of convention. In other words, the business letter is written the way it is written because that's the way it is *always* written, and there is not much point in arguing about it.

At first, the idea of writing in a conventional manner may seem restricting. Why not "stand out from the crowd" by hand-writing your letter in red ink; why not write it on the back of an 8 × 10 glossy photograph of yourself? The answer is: because these creative approaches are not established business practice. The business letter format is not the place to be creative; it is the responsibility of the business person to know proper business letter format and follow it. Save inventiveness for the content of the letter.

Whether you're applying for a job on a construction crew or as a hospital orderly, the person hiring you wants to see some indication that you know how things are done at a construction site or in a hospital and that you are willing to go along with established practice. Your potential employer will have to work with you. Will you turn out to be the kind of person who argues over every detail and challenges every rule? Are you so "green" that you will have to have everything explained to you? If you give that impression, your potential boss may decide that it would be easier to work with someone else.

A business letter creates an impression of who you are and what you know. You want your letter to show that you will be easy to train and work with, that you will be an asset to the employer, not a liability. Again, following accepted practice, including conventional letter formatting, is just another, subtle way of demonstrating a service attitude.

Stationery

For most business purposes, $8\frac{1}{2}'' \times 11''$, unlined white paper is appropriate. Never use onionskin or erasable paper for business letters. Instead, ask for 20-pound or 16-pound *bond* stationery, that is, a heavy-grade or high-quality paper, usually with some rag content (cloth fiber) in addition to wood pulp. Quality paper costs more, but it will make a better impression than cheaper paper. Be sure to buy envelopes of the same type and quality; and, while you're at the stationery store, pick up a new ribbon for your typewriter (black only). All business letters should be typed (or created on a word processor), single-spaced, and the type should be dark and easy to read. Don't use script or other fancy typefaces. The less the format of the letter calls attention to itself, the better. After all, it's the message that you want the reader to remember.

Some experts in the job-search field recommend the smaller Monarch-sized ($7\frac{1}{2}'' \times 10\frac{1}{2}''$) stationery. Their theory is that the writer should be trying to write concisely. Short letters receive more attention than long ones, and short letters fit better on this slightly smaller paper. Also, Monarch-sized paper makes the letter stand out from those written on $8\frac{1}{2}'' \times 11''$, Executive-sized paper. Others argue that Executive-sized paper is easier for the employer to handle and fits better into company files. Again, thinking of what might be most convenient for the potential employer is a subtle example of the service attitude.

To make the letter more memorable, some experts also recommend stationery in colors other than white, say a subtle gray, ivory, or beige. The choice of color and size is up to you, but remember: if you decide to deviate from standard business practice, make sure you have a good reason for doing so—and don't go too far.

Six parts of the business letter

Every standard business letter has these six parts: the heading, the inside address, the salutation, the body, the complimentary close, and the signature block. The letter may have other elements, such as an attention line or an enclosure notation. Take a look at the sample letter on the following page to familiarize yourself with standard format. The six parts common to all letters are labeled in italics on the right side of the letter.

The **heading** consists of the address of the person sending the letter (but not his or her name) and the date. If letterhead stationery is used—that is, stationery on which your name, address, and telephone number have been printed by a professional printer—the heading will consist only of the date. Always include the ZIP code as part of the heading address.

```
1269 Gilmore Drive                                             heading
Decatur, Illinois 62522
February 9, 1989



Mr. Robert W. Watson                                       inside address
Operations Manager
Carter Manufacturing, Inc.
271 E. Thirty-fourth St.
Chicago, Illinois 60657

Dear Mr. Watson:                                              salutation

First, let me say how much I enjoyed touring Carter Manufacturing
with you after our interview last Friday.  Seeing the facility
firsthand gave me a much clearer idea of both the manufacturing
process and the organization of personnel within the plant.  I
appreciate your taking time to show me around.                  body


Thanks, too, for recommending that I also visit with James Dieter
at Staymac Corporation.  I phoned his office right after our
visit, and I have an appointment to see him next week.  I'm sure
that the information he has agreed to provide, coupled with what
I learned in talking with you, will help me a great deal in
completing my senior report.


   Sincerely,                                          complimentary close



   William F. Kennedy                                      signature block
```

If the letter must continue on a second sheet of paper, the heading for the second page and subsequent pages consists of the name of the person to whom the letter is being written, the page number, and the date. Two formats for second-page headings are acceptable:

Mr. Robert W. Watson   -2-   February 9, 1989

or:

Mr. Robert W. Watson
February 9, 1989
Page 2

Letterhead is not used for the second and subsequent pages of the letter, and the sender's address need not appear on subsequent pages.

The **inside address** is the address of the person to whom the letter is being sent. Notice in the sample letter that the person's job title (Operations Manager) is included in the address, and so is the name of the firm for which he works. Notice, too, that a polite title precedes the person's name: *Mr.* Robert W. Watson. Other polite titles are: Miss, Mrs., Ms., Dr., Rev. (note that *Miss* is not followed by a period, whereas *Mrs.* is).

The **salutation** is simply the greeting: "Dear . . ." It almost always includes the person's polite title, followed by his or her last name only and a colon. If you know the person to whom you are writing very well, and it seems appropriate to do so, you may use his or her first name only: "Dear Bob." In this case, the colon is replaced by a comma. Do not put yourself on a first-name basis with someone in a letter, however, unless you enjoy that same relationship face-to-face.

It's usually preferable to write to a specific person by name rather than to begin the letter "Dear Personnel Manager" or "To Whom It May Concern." On some occasions, however, the letter is general and addressed to the organization itself. In those cases, the salutation has traditionally been "Dear Gentlemen" or simply "Gentlemen." Because of the growing awareness that not all business people are men, however, the salutation "Dear Gentlemen/Ladies" is sometimes adopted. Some writers find this approach awkward, and instead use the company name: "Dear Carter Manufacturing." Which do you think works better in these circumstances?

The **body** of the letter is the message. It is single-spaced and, unless the letter is very short, divided into paragraphs. More will be said in later chapters about how to compose the body of the letter.

The **complimentary close** is, in effect, a "sign-off" signal which assures the reader of your sincerity, honesty, truthfulness, or good will. This is why traditional complimentary closes are: "Sincerely," "Yours truly," "Faithfully yours," "Cordially yours," "Respectfully," and the like.

The **signature block** consists of the typed name of the letter writer and his or her title if any. So, the signature block of a letter from Robert Watson would look like this:

Robert W. Watson
Operations Manager

Occasionally, for reasons of legal liability, letter writers may wish to make it clear that they are writing on behalf of the firm and not personally. In that case, the complimentary close and signature block might look like this:

Very truly yours,

CARTER MANUFACTURING, INC.

Robert W. Watson

Robert W. Watson
Operations Manager

Other elements of the business letter

Every business letter should contain the six parts just discussed. A letter might also contain one or more of the following elements: an attention line, a subject line, the initials of the dictator and typist, an enclosure notation, a copy notation, or a postscript. The next sample letter incorporates these additional elements. Again, the elements of the letter—the basic six parts and additional parts—are labeled in italics on the right side. This is a letter *about* a job applicant rather than *from* an applicant. Notice that, because it is written on Mrs. Rowan's company letterhead, the heading of the letter consists of the *dateline* only. Notice, too, the second-page heading on this example of a two-page letter.

The **attention line** is inserted just after the inside address and before the salutation. It is often used when the letter is addressed to a large organization but the writer wants a particular person to read it. The writer may or may not know the name of the person.

The **subject line** appears after the salutation. Its purpose is to tell the reader quickly what the letter is about. Sometimes the subject line refers to past correspondence or to a file number or order number. Thus, it helps the reader understand the context in which the letter was written. It also makes the letter easier for the reader to file. To make the subject line stand out, writers often put it in capital letters or underline it. The subject line may also be centered in the middle of the line. Sometimes the word "subject" is omitted, or the word "about" is substituted. Some writers still use the conventional "re" for "regarding," as in: "Re: Mary Beth Livey."

The **initials** at the bottom of the page indicate that Mrs. Rowan (PR) dictated the letter and that someone with the initials jld typed it. Here, the dictator's initials are capital letters and the typist's initials are lowercase letters. But any typographical form that indicates who's who is acceptable: PR/jld, pr/jld, PR:JLD. The initials serve as a record of the correspondence for the sender and aren't of much interest to the reader.

The **enclosure notation** directs the reader to look for something additional in the letter: a resume, a photo, a document, a clipping. Sometimes the word "enclosure" is spelled out, and sometimes the number of items enclosed is noted, as in: "Enc.: 2."

The **copy notation** is of interest to the reader because it indicates who else has read the letter. In this example, Mrs. Rowan has sent a copy of the correspondence to her boss, Mr. Baylor. The notation is both a record of

BAYLOR, SMITH & WILEY, INC.

Public Relations and Corporate Marketing
129 Statton Building, Suite A
Tallahassee, Florida 32306

(202) 555-8979

June 7, 1989   *dateline*

Compton-Smith, Publishers
889 Greenwood Blvd.   *inside address*
Tallahassee, Florida 32306

Attention: Personnel Department   *attention line*

Gentlemen/Ladies: *salutation*

SUBJECT: Mary Beth Livey   *subject line*

I am forwarding to you work performance review sheets and
additional material concerning a young woman who worked for us as
an intern during her senior year at the University of Florida.
Mary Beth Livey worked under my direction as an account coordinator from January 17 through April 5 of this year. She
graduated, with honors, I understand, this spring and she is
currently seeking employment.

As you may know, our firm specializes in health services industry
corporations; two of the local hospitals and a local hospital
supply firm are clients of ours. Several prominent physicians
also retain us. Ms. Livey was primarily a market researcher for
us. Among other projects, she completed an extensive report on
the women's health care market, which was especially well
received. I have enclosed a copy of this report to give you an
idea of the scope and quality of her work. Her duties also
included client liaison and some ad copywriting, for which she
seems to have a particular talent.

                                               body

My associates and I were very impressed with Ms. Livey, as the
enclosed work performance reviews indicate. Everyone found her
to be hardworking and pleasant. As her immediate superior, I had
many opportunities to observe her on the job. She is quick to
learn new tasks and poised in the company of clients. She is
diligent and careful in her research and an excellent writer.

Ms. Livey has told me of her interest in the publishing business
and of her intention to seek employment with your firm; she has
asked me to write to you in her behalf and forward the enclosed
confidential performance reviews. She will, no doubt, be
contacting your department soon for an interview. I certainly
feel she would be an asset to any business, and I urge you to
consider her application.

Sincerely,   *complimentary close*

(Mrs.) Phyllis Rowan
Account Executive   *signature block*

PR/jld   *initials*
Enc.   *enclosure notation*
c: William Baylor   *copy notation*

P.S. You are free to photocopy any of the enclosed material for
your files, but we will need to have both the review sheets and
the report returned to us.
                                                    postscript

that fact (and a reminder to the secretary to send a copy to the person designated) and a notice to the personnel department of Compton-Smith that Mr. Baylor also knows the contents of the letter.

The **postscript** is, supposedly, an afterthought, that is, an addition to the message of the letter. But in a well-planned letter, there should be nothing left out, no important information that must be tacked on to the end of the letter. Postscripts, therefore, do not often appear in business letters, except in sales letters. Because postscripts attract attention and are often read before the letter in which they appear, they are the perfect place for a salesperson to make an emphatic pitch. For example: "Remember, you have only five days to take advantage of this fabulous offer!" In general, avoid postscripts, but if you must use one, make it short and use the initials P.S. to indicate that the addition is a postscript.

Forms of indentation

Like every other human endeavor, letter writing has changed over the years. Once, business correspondence was a highly formal matter, and business people often closed their letters with a phrase such as "I remain your servant, . . ." Business people today are not as formal—nor as servile—and today's trend is toward speed and simplicity.

The two letters you have studied thus far in the chapter are written in what is called the *full-block* format; that is, every line begins at the extreme left margin, with no indentations for paragraphs. This format is fast because the typist doesn't need to take time to indent. The page has an efficient look.

In the *modified-block* format, the inside address (or dateline if the letter is written on letterhead stationery), the complimentary close, and the signature block are aligned at the center of the page, but paragraphs are not indented. In the *semi-block* format, this same alignment of elements is used, but the paragraphs are also indented. There is also an almost outmoded format, called *indented,* in which both paragraphs and each line in the inside address and signature block are indented.

The sample letter on the next page is written in the modified-block format. Compare it to the full-block letters on pages 75 and 78-79. Which format do you prefer and why? Can you identify each element of the letter?

779 West Fifty-sixth St.
New York, NY 10103
March 21, 1989

Hollowell and Bennet, Inc.
44 East Fifty-first St.
New York, NY 10128

Attention Order Department

Gentlemen:

Purchase Order No. 59242

On February 3, I ordered a textbook entitled <u>Basic Computer Programming</u> from your firm and prepaid the order, plus shipping costs, in order to receive the book as quickly as possible. To date, however, I have received neither the book nor any correspondence from you that might explain the delay.

Would you please check your records and let me know if the book has been shipped.

Yours truly,

William Fogarty

WF/grc

Punctuation

If you were to study business letter writing more thoroughly, you would find variation not only in the way writers indent elements of the letter, but also in the way they punctuate. The most traditional—some would say old-fashioned—format for punctuation requires a comma or period after each line of the heading and inside address and after each line of the signature block. This format is called *closed* punctuation, and is illustrated below.

As you can see, this format requires more effort to type than more streamlined punctuation styles; for that reason, it is not used much today. The other extreme in punctuation is called *open* punctuation. In that format, no punctuation follows the salutation or complimentary close. Only the commas and periods grammatically required in the headings (between the city and state, for example) or in the body of the letter appear in open-punctuation letters.

Mixed Punctuation

Closed Punctuation

Open Punctuation

The middle-of-the-road punctuation style is called *mixed* punctuation. This style requires a colon after the salutation (or a comma if the salutation uses the reader's first name) and a comma after the complimentary close.

Companies vary as to punctuation and indentation formats, and you will, of course, adopt the style your firm uses once you get a job. For job application and other job-search letters, it's best to stick to mixed punctuation and full-block, modified-block, or semi-block indentation.

Your turn

Now that you have some familiarity with letter formats, write a letter in the semi-block style (modified-block but with indented paragraphs), using mixed punctuation. Type or write on 8½" × 11", unlined white paper. Imagine that you are complaining to a company, as William Fogarty did, or asking for information. Include all the elements of business letters that you have studied (attention line, copy notation, salutation, and so on) and label them.

Questions for discussion

1. Some experts in the job-search field recommend that job seekers purchase personal letterhead stationery. Some experts also recommend that job seekers have business cards printed. Do you think these measures would impress a potential employer, or would they make the job seeker seem pretentious?

2. If a woman does not specify whether she is Miss or Mrs., how should you address her? Suppose you received a letter from a D. J. Peterson and did not know whether Peterson was a man or a woman. How would you write back to that person? Is there any tactful way to determine which title is appropriate?

3. The complimentary close may seem like a mere formality, but the words there carry meaning, too. What is the difference in connotation between "Cordially yours" and "Respectfully yours," for example, or "Sincerely" and "Yours truly"? Which would be most appropriate for writing to your priest, rabbi, or minister? Which for your favorite uncle? Which would be most appropriate for a letter of complaint to a department store? Which for a job application letter? What would be the effect of having no complimentary close? Can you think of situations where it might be appropriate not to include one?

8 The application letter as a sales letter

You probably receive at least one or two sales letters a week, letters asking you to purchase merchandise, subscribe to a magazine, or donate to a cause. You may not want to take advantage of every "incredible offer" these letters contain, and you may not be able to afford the "gigantic savings" they promise; but you can learn a great deal about how to write business letters from studying what works — and what doesn't — in direct mail advertising.

Action as the purpose of business letters

In a sense, almost every business letter is a sales letter. Of course, some letters are written simply to pass along information. But the purpose of most business letters is to promote some kind of action. The writer wants the reader to do something: buy a product, accept a decision, pay a bill. The writer's attempts to persuade the reader to do these things amount to a kind of sales pitch. In the case of job application letters, the writer wants the reader to grant an interview, that is, to "spend" his or her time in talking with the applicant.

The resume alone usually will not sell your qualifications (no product sells itself). The resume is simply raw data, an objective record of your background. True, an employer *might* interview or even hire you on the basis of your resume alone. But the better the job, the more the employer will want to see how your unique blend of qualifications (listed on the resume) and personal qualities (demonstrated in the letter and interview) fit together to make you the ideal applicant.

The application letter demonstrates your command of proper job application procedures as well as your ability to take charge, ask for the job you want, and prove you deserve to get it. No matter how good your background is, the job market is so crowded that an employer will probably receive several resumes just as impressive as yours. How can you prove that you are special? The answer is: by spotlighting certain facets of your experience and training that *particularly* suit you for the job. Your letter will argue that there is a match between the job requirements and the experience and training indicated on your resume. By writing a skillful letter, tailored to a particular job situation, you will *persuade* the employer to grant you an interview.

Persuasion

Suppose you are in the furniture business and you have to sell 100 sofas by the end of the month or go broke. Your customers may feel sorry for you, but your financial desperation won't persuade them to buy a sofa. Keeping you in black ink is not to *their* benefit. Likewise, potential employers may genuinely sympathize with you if you are having trouble finding employment, but telling them your troubles won't persuade them to give you a job.

In most cases, people act not for someone else's benefit but for their own. You must provide an incentive to your customers in order to sell the sofas: a twenty percent discount on the selling price, low interest rates, a free lamp with every sofa purchased, free delivery. All these are benefits to your customers and might persuade them to buy. Likewise, in a job application letter you must show the employer that it is in his or her interests to interview you.

Persuasion is like the service attitude discussed in Chapter 1; it involves putting yourself in the other person's position and imagining what that other person wants. Letters are an abstract form of communication, but don't forget that a real, live human being is eventually going to read what you write. Chances are, he or she will be a lot like you and will want the same sort of honest and respectful treatment you would want. You would not be persuaded to a course of action by a letter that tried to manipulate you or one that insulted your intelligence or bored you to tears. Neither will your reader. Write sincerely. Write with your reader's interests in mind. Write a letter that you yourself would like to receive, and that letter will usually impress the reader, too.

Standard three-part business letter organization

It's helpful to think of the business letter as consisting of three blocks of information. Call them A, B, and C; why, what, and when; the beginning, middle, and end; the opening, body, and conclusion; or whatever. No matter what they're called, the three parts always function in the same way.

The **opening** of the letter (usually just one short paragraph) tells why you are writing. It should be direct and specific. It should also reflect a strong service attitude and, when possible, offer the promise of some benefit to the reader. Remember, few readers are *obliged* to read your letter. As the writer, your job is to make the opening paragraph so interesting that the reader feels compelled to keep reading, and what's more interesting to people than news of something of benefit to themselves?

The **body** of the letter is the message. Here, arguments are advanced and situations are explained. The length of this section is determined by the complexity of the letter's message, but good writers always resist the temptation to write too much.

Within the body of the letter, information should be presented in some sort of order. State the problem, for example, then the solution. Pose a question; then answer it. Or use a chronological organizational pattern to give the history of a situation. If necessary, outline the contents of the body of the letter before you write so that you are sure you are presenting information in a logical sequence.

The **conclusion** of the letter reaffirms the service attitude and usually asks the reader to take some action or specifies what action the writer will take and when. For example: "Please contact our office for an appointment as soon as possible." Or: "I will consult with the board of directors on the matter this week and notify you of our decision." Notice that the action requested or promised is specific and stated directly. If you can specify a time for the action, all the better.

Model sales letter

Take a look at the model sales letter on the following page. Notice that the letter divides into three parts and that each part is designed to achieve a particular communication goal.

Whatever you may think of the writing style of this sales letter, you must admit that the content is well organized. Notice that in the opening (first paragraph), the writer flatters the reader a bit ("good customers like you") and outlines a potential benefit to the reader ("special opportunity to save"). In the body of the letter (second and third paragraphs), the writer explains the benefit further, arranging details in a logical sequence: how the savings is made possible, what the savings is, what is offered in addition to the savings.

In the conclusion (fourth paragraph), the writer specifies exactly what the reader should do ("stop by") and when ("now"). Notice, too, that the writer gives the reader additional reasons for acting and acting quickly ("selection is still good," "offer ends June 30"). Finally, the writer displays a service attitude ("happy to demonstrate . . . and to arrange . . .").

ACME FURNITURE COMPANY
149 Easton Road, Philadelphia PA 19103
(215) 555-9708

June 2, 1989

Mr. Fred Carroll
2918 Bradley Ave.
Philadelphia PA 19125

Dear Mr. Carroll:

Here at Acme Furniture Company, we value good customers like you, and we want to keep them coming back. That's why we're offering you a special opportunity to save on quality furniture during the month of June.

Our volume buying policy has again allowed us to make a special purchase of beautiful Brannigan sofas and matching chairs at an unheard-of low price, and during the month of June we'll be passing the savings along to you. These finely crafted sofas come in the latest styles and fabrics, and they are being offered to our special customers at the unbelievable price of just $399.

This price will not be advertised until July. But we're offering this bargain to special customers now. And there's more. With each Brannigan sofa sold, we're offering, free, a color-coordinated Fairhall lamp. That's a $59 value, absolutely free, if you buy during the month of June.

So stop by now, while the selection is still good, and ask one of our sales people to show you the beautiful Brannigan line. We'll be happy to demonstrate the quality features of Brannigan and to arrange convenient terms should you decide to buy. Prices will never be lower, and remember, the free Fairhall lamp offer ends June 30.

Cordially,

ACME FURNITURE COMPANY

John Jordan
Sales Representative

Review

Understanding the standard three-part business letter organizational pattern can be an important job-search tool for you as you attempt to sell your qualifications in a job application letter. And it can help you write business letters once you get a job, because almost any business letter situation can be organized into the same three-part pattern. To make sure you understand the function of each part of the standard business letter, take a minute now to review the pattern. In the spaces provided here, jot down the function of each of the three parts of a standard business letter. When you have completed this exercise, turn to the end of the chapter for additional discussion of the pattern.

1. *The opening.* _____
_____
_____
_____

2. *The body.* _____
_____
_____
_____

3. *The conclusion.* _____
_____
_____
_____

Applying sales letter organization to the job application letter

Having studied the sales letter from Acme Furniture Company, you could probably write one just as good, selling imaginary used cars or vacuum cleaners. The only trouble is, you're not selling *things,* you're selling *yourself.* You don't want to sell your skills at bargain prices; and, obviously, you can't give away a free lamp with every job offer. How, then, *can* you persuade potential employers that they would benefit by interviewing you?

The opening

It may help to realize that a large part of your letter is already somewhat organized. At least, you have your goals in mind. You know exactly what action you want the reader to take, for instance: you want him or her to telephone or write to you to set up an interview. You also know—having done some thinking about your qualifications and some research about the company to which you are applying—several good reasons why you should be interviewed. Your biggest problem, then, is writing the opening paragraph.

The opening of the job application letter is crucial. Not every job application letter gets read. If the letter's format or the tone or approach of the first paragraph is wrong, the employer may not bother to read on. Remember, employers are trying to narrow the field of applicants down to one as fast as possible.

Here are three opening paragraphs for job application letters. If you were an employer, which would persuade you to read the letter all the way through? Which letters would you discard unread and why? After you have judged the opening paragraphs for yourself, turn to the end of the chapter for a discussion of their effectiveness.

1. Dear Sir,

   I am writing to you about the job in the paper. I have a degree in chemical engineering and one year of experience.

2. Dear Mr. Reilly:

   I believe I have the qualifications necessary to be the best salesman your firm ever employed. I have three years of experience selling sports equipment with Carver Sports and Recreation, Inc. in Madison, Wisconsin. My resume is enclosed.

3. Dear Mrs. Atley,

   I recently graduated from Kirkland Polytechnical Institute with a degree in hotel management. I would like to find a position as an assistant manager or similar position in a major hotel chain so that I can add to my education with on-the-job training. I would prefer the West Coast, but would be willing to work anywhere at first.

If you have understood the principles discussed so far in this book — the service attitude; the importance of persuasion; the need for specific, focused information and correct format — you probably weren't enthusiastic about any of these letter openings. Here's a much better one:

Dear Mr. Atkinson:

   As a recent graduate of the diesel mechanics program at Farley Technical Institute, I believe I have the training and experience to fill the position of maintenance mechanic for which you advertised in last Sunday's *Chicago Tribune*.

This opening paragraph is concise and specific; it is confident without being arrogant. Assuming Farley Technical Institute is a reputable school — one that provides the kind of training necessary for the job of maintenance mechanic — and assuming the rest of the letter is as straightforward and impressive as this first paragraph, the employer would probably interview this applicant.

The body

In the body of the letter you will present your evidence — selected and spot-lighted portions of your enclosed resume that show you are particularly right for the job. The evidence should be arranged in some sort of logical order so that your argument will be easy for the reader to follow. Here's one that, like many resumes, uses an organizational pattern of reverse chronology:

As the enclosed resume shows, I specialized in diesel mechanics at Farley and earned an overall grade point average of 3.2. Before I enrolled in Farley, however, I had worked for two years as a service station attendant and part-time mechanic for Ray's Standard Service on Interstate 80 south of town. My work there gave me my first opportunity to work on diesels and convinced me that I wanted a career as a diesel mechanic.

There are, no doubt, dozens of diesel mechanics graduates from Farley Technical Institute, but not all, like this applicant, earned good grades. And not all, like this graduate, have practical experience. A busy employer, looking over dozens of resumes, might be tempted to view the applicant as "just another Farley graduate." But the letter separates this applicant from the crowd by emphasizing additional selling points from the resume. Notice, too, that the writer *expresses* interest in the field of diesel mechanics rather than leaving it to be assumed by the reader.

The conclusion

So far, so good. The letter has shown the applicant to be businesslike and well qualified for the job. Now the writer is ready to nail down an interview in which to "close the sale." The conclusion of an application letter should specifically *ask* for an interview. Don't leave any room for misunderstanding by assuming the employer will understand that you want to be interviewed.

You might want to follow up the request with a promise to telephone the employer's office. This is a take-charge strategy that puts you in an active role instead of in the passive position of waiting for the employer to call. He or she may misplace your application or just put off contacting you, and that leaves you up in the air. Showing determination is appropriate, but don't be pushy.

Finally, try to express the service attitude in the conclusion (without fawning, of course) and make sure you give the impression that you want the job. Here's an example of a well-written concluding paragraph:

I'm very interested in a position with your firm and would welcome the opportunity to talk with you personally about my qualifications. I work from 8 a.m. to noon every day, but could be available at any time convenient for you after noon. I will telephone your office next week to see if it is possible to set up an interview appointment.

Your turn

Now that you have studied letter formatting in Chapter 7 and business letter organization in this chapter, try writing your own application letter. Use 8$\frac{1}{2}$″ × 11″ unlined white paper, and type the letter if possible, making it as correct and persuasive as you would if you were going to send it to an employer.

Then trade your letter for a classmate's. Acting as the employer, evaluate the other person's letter. Write comments on it indicating what is effective and what is not and then return it. When you receive your own letter back, study it carefully. Are your classmate's comments accurate and fair? Rewrite the letter to improve it; and, again, have a classmate evaluate it for you.

Discussion of chapter exercises

Review of standard three-part organizational pattern, page 89

The opening of the letter should be direct, specific, and interesting. It should make the reader want to read on. If possible, it should mention something of benefit to the reader. In sales letters, this is often something tangible: a bargain, a free gift. In most letters, however, the benefit or positive aspect of the opening is more abstract: a compliment, a promise to help the reader, an interesting fact. Writers should not let a preoccupation with benefit to the reader twist the opening of the letter. Benefits should not be contrived. The main thing to remember is not to annoy the reader with vague, boring, or phony statements. Often, the benefit to themselves that readers perceive in a well-written opening is simply that they are reading the letter of someone who knows what he or she is doing, someone who will not waste the reader's time.

The body of the letter presents the details, the argument, the explanation. The main thing to remember in writing this part of the letter is that some sort of organizational pattern should be operating: question and answer, problem and solution, chronological organization, or the like.

The conclusion of the letter should leave no loose ends or unanswered questions. The writer should state specifically what he or she intends to do and when, or what he or she wants the reader to do and when.

Analysis of letter openings, page 90

1. It is obvious that the writer is writing to the reader, so the first sentence here is boring and unnecessary. Although the opening sentence of a job application letter doesn't have to be a real "grabber," it should have more life to it than this one.

The rest of the information is not specific enough: a degree from what school, experience where? Being specific is a cardinal rule of any business letter, and of communication in general.

If a job application letter is written in response to an invitation to apply—as here, where the job was advertised in a newspaper—the writer should state the name of the job he or she is applying for and the name and edition date of the newspaper in which it was advertised. Large companies may advertise every week, and they may advertise more than one position at a time. If that were the case here, the reader would not be able to identify the job to which the writer was referring.

Finally, the letter should be written to a specific person if possible, or at least to a specific job title, as in: "Dear Personnel Manager." The salutation should be punctuated with a colon rather than a comma.

2. This is better. The format is correct, and the writer took the trouble to find out the name of the person to whom the letter should be addressed. But if the resume is enclosed, won't that be obvious to the reader? Rather than tell the reader something he already knows or can find out for himself, it would have been better to refer to the resume indirectly. For example: "As the enclosed resume shows, I have three years of experience in this field."

The writer's opening sentence, if true, would certainly promise a benefit for the employer. You decide whether it is confident or boastful.

3. Here the purpose of the letter is not clear. Why is the writer telling the reader all this information (the writer knows, but the reader doesn't)? The application letter is a matter of matching relevant qualifications to a specific job. This paragraph needs to be focused, and irrelevant information—where the applicant would prefer to work—cut out. Suggested rewrite: "As a recent graduate in hotel management from Kirkland Polytechnical Institute, I am very interested in the position of assistant manager which you advertised in the *New York Times* on May 23."

9 Handling problems and establishing a businesslike tone

As you learned in the last chapter, the application letter—also sometimes called a cover letter because it accompanies or "covers" a resume—has three functions:

1. To generate interest in your application
2. To highlight the best selling points in your resume
3. To secure an interview

There are two types of application letters: invited and unsolicited. Invited application letters are like those you studied in Chapter 8; they are written in response to a company's advertisement or some other sort of invitation to apply. When campus recruiters visit a school and conduct interviews, for example, the company the recruiter represents is inviting you to apply for employment. The same is true when a potential employer suggests to you verbally that you submit an application. In other words, if you know that a specific job exists or you know that a firm is currently hiring people, your application would be invited.

In these circumstances, as you learned in the previous chapter, the opening of your letter can be fairly straightforward. You simply say what job you are applying for, how you heard about the opening, and what qualifies you for the job.

However, most jobs—some experts claim as many as seventy-five percent—are not advertised. College and university students are fortunate when recruiters from large companies conduct interviews on campus because, as a rule, employers don't pursue applicants. As you learned in Chapter 2, waiting for an opportunity to apply—relying on the newspaper classified ads to turn up a job, for example—is not the best way to go about looking for work. So, many of the job application letters you write will be unsolicited.

Tailoring the opening for unsolicited applications

Unsolicited job application letters—also called prospecting letters—are written when no job with the firm in question has been advertised or otherwise mentioned to you. These letters are harder to write than invited letters because you approach the company cold, with no "introduction."

Your job, therefore, is to make it seem as though you have a particular reason for applying, a reason beyond the mere fact that you need a job. Think of the telephone solicitors who call you with news of a special sale or a free gift. They always have a "hook" or gimmick—some special reason why they called. Your opening paragraph, it is hoped, will not be as transparent or obnoxious as the usual telephone sales pitch, but it will be designed to accomplish the same goal: to break the ice and establish a relationship between you and the person to whom you are writing.

So, why *did* you decide to apply to this particular company? You may have picked the firm's name out of the phone book; but chances are, even if you did, you still had some reason for writing the firm. Do you know someone who works there? Have you used the firm's products or services? Have you read about the firm or heard someone talking about it recently? Any of these circumstances could furnish an opening for an unsolicited job application letter. Here are three examples:

1. Dear Miss Windsor:

   I was very interested in the talk you gave at the Hanover Public Library last week, especially your discussion of the current opportunities in your own field of real estate investment. I'll be graduating from university soon, and I'd like very much to visit with you about possible job openings at Windsor Realty.

2. Dear Mr. Olson:

   During the summer of 1988, I worked on the loading dock at Olson Manufacturing. I liked my job, especially the foreman, Pete Riggs. He was a great guy. The work was easy and paid well. I'm wondering if you currently have any jobs open.

3. Dear Ms. Ryan:

   It's impossible these days to pick up a newspaper or turn on a radio without hearing about your highly successful company, Addison/Ryan, Inc. Your example is an inspiration to people like me who dream of starting their own business. Could I possibly talk with you personally about opportunities at Addison/Ryan?

Tone

As you can see from the three examples just given, the problem in writing the opening of an unsolicited application letter is to devise something true and interesting to say without going overboard. In other words, it is a problem of *tone*.

Tone is the attitude the writer takes toward the reader and the subject matter. If a writer holds himself superior to his reader, for example, his tone might be described as condescending. If a writer does not take her subject seriously, her tone might be considered humorous or ironic. If a writer tries to flatter the reader in order to gain some advantage, the tone will be fawning and insincere. Tone can be described as formal, casual, mocking, sincere, contemptuous, indifferent; in short, tone reflects the whole range of human attitudes.

The best way to assure good tone in a business letter is to assume that your reader is as bright, courteous, and sophisticated as you are — but no more so. Of course, some people deserve your special respect. The potential employer is one of them. But, in general, you should treat the reader as an equal. That way, you are not likely to seem either fawning or condescending.

Skillful writers can control the tone of their writing through their choice of words, their selection of examples and illustrations, their organization, their use of active or passive voice, even their punctuation. In other words, their writing accurately reflects their good attitude toward their readers and their subjects. But less skillful writers sometimes unintentionally convey the wrong tone.

Among the best ways to destroy good tone is to use tricks or blatant flattery; the reader almost always sees through these strategies and is rightfully offended by them. Here are a few more ways a writer might thoughtlessly alienate the reader.

Telling readers something they already know

Reading what you already know is boring. Further, it's insulting when someone explains information to you that is common knowledge. If you think you have to state some obvious piece of information, do it in an indirect way. Don't write, for example: "Spring is almost here, and you will soon be sending interviewers to McFarland Vocational College, where I am currently enrolled." The reader knows what season it is and what his or her plans are.

Instead, write: "When you visit McFarland Vocational College this spring, I hope you will grant me some additional time to take you on a tour of the lab facilities where I am conducting my senior research project." Instead of writing: "You interviewed me on July 8," write: "When you interviewed me on July 8, . . ." In other words, just refresh the reader's memory, subtly.

A good strategy is to demonstrate in your letter that you know something about the reader's firm, but use care in how you phrase your sentences. Imagine, for example, how a corporate executive might respond to a statement like this one: "Your company, which began as a small family business in Maryland, has grown rapidly over the past thirty years and is now one of the top three in its field." A more tactful writer might allude to his or her knowledge of the company indirectly and express instead a reaction to that knowledge: "When I read the history of Taylor Manufacturing recently in *Time* magazine, I was impressed with the company's rapid growth. I knew I wanted to be a part of such an organization."

Choosing a tone that is too personal or too formal

Do not let your respect for the reader, your concern for the conventions of the business world, or your desire to sound impressive twist your writing into stiff, stuffy posturing. Phrases such as "Pertinent action will be forthcoming" or "In regard to your letter of the fifth, please be advised . . ." are not classy. Rather, they suggest a cold indifference to the reader. It's acceptable, even advisable, to use a few contractions ("can't," "won't," "I'm") to soften your writing. Everyday language (but not slang) is appropriate, too. Just don't go overboard.

On the other hand, don't be too informal. Overly friendly writing makes readers defensive; they know you are trying to manipulate them. Writing that is too personal will make the writer seem silly and incompetent.

Be especially careful in using the reader's name. Such phrasing as "Since you are, Mr. Smith, a leader in the community, . . ." smacks of fawning. The inside address indicates that the letter is addressed to Smith; there is no need to repeat his name in the letter's body. Never use the reader's first name unless you know him or her *very* well, and never jump to using a nickname unless the person in question asks you to do so.

Exaggerating

The best way to impress the reader is to use facts — specific facts, presented with a minimum of editorial comment. If you earned a straight A average in your major, that fact speaks for itself. Any employer will recognize the significance of your accomplishment. Don't write: "In college, I distinguished myself in academic excellence by earning a straight A average." Just write: "In college, I earned a straight A average."

Likewise, avoid superlatives such as "best" and "greatest" unless they are factual statements. The following, for example, is a statement of fact: "I was voted best debater by an interuniversity council." But this statement is a value judgment and could be construed as bragging: "I worked with the greatest teacher in the world, and I turned out to be one of his best students." Think of your own reaction when advertisers tell you their product is "amazing," "revolutionary," or "perfect." Overstating the case almost always makes the reader doubt your word.

On the other hand, don't be humble. Be on guard for any natural inclination you may have to downplay your qualifications. Treat yourself and your accomplishments with the respect they honestly deserve. Again, if you stick to the facts, you will not be bothered by the uncomfortable feeling that you are bragging.

Accusing the reader

Language can be tricky. It's easy to seem to imply something you don't really mean. Take this statement, for example: "I'm sorry I missed our appointment. Your office neglected to inform me of the time and date." Doesn't it imply that the reader's office is not very efficient? Or this statement: "I can't understand why you failed to interview me. Other companies were eager to talk with me." On the surface, the writer is saying that he or she is puzzled. But the implication is that the reader's actions don't make sense ("I can't understand . . ."), that he or she has "failed," and that he or she is out of step with what other employers are doing.

If you must point out a reader's mistake or shortcoming, do so indirectly or take the blame yourself. For example: "I'm sorry I missed our appointment. I'm afraid I didn't remember to check the exact time with your office." Or simply sweep the matter under the rug and go on: "I'm sorry I missed our appointment. Can we set up a time to talk next week?"

4950 Fifty-fourth St., Apt. 3
Nashville, TN 37203
April 5, 1989

Mrs. G. Lynn Brown
Director of Research
Colson Foods, Inc.
698 Redpath Road
Memphis, TN 36111

Dear Mrs. Brown

As a student at Hinsdale Polytechnical Institute, I often had
occasion to write to and visit Colson Foods to collect research
information for school papers, and I was always impressed with
the plant and the people who worked there.

Soon I will be graduating from Hinsdale with a degree in
Nutrition and Diet and would like to find a job in nutrition
research.

As the enclosed resume indicates, I specialized in research
during my four years at Hinsdale and completed three independent
research projects. I am especially interested in "substitute"
products like egg and salt substitutes which might help Americans
control their diet better and thus, live a longer and more
healthy life. I have very personal reasons for my interest in
this field.

I would appreciate an interview at your convenience.

Sincerely

Virginia G. Morton

Virginia G. Morton

Craig Allen
3341 Dubuque St.
Iowa City, IA 52240
November 21, 1988

Mr. I. G. Goldstein
Director of Student Affairs
Room 122, Andover Hall
University of Iowa
Iowa City, Iowa 52244

Dear Mr. Goldstein:

When Jeff Wilson graduates next spring, you're going to be
looking for a new student assistant. I'd like to get my "hat in
the ring" early because I really want the job of assistant to the
Director of Student Affairs.

What qualifies me? Well, as a member of TKO fraternity,
I'm active in Greek life on campus and know most of the other
fraternity and sorority members. I've served one year as
president of TKO and a semester on the Greek Life Committee. I'm
active--though not outstanding--in U. of I. sports, and I'm a
member of several campus organizations, including the Photography
Club. I know your office publishes a quarterly newsletter, and
I'm sure my ability to photograph campus events would be useful.

I think I could be the kind of liaison person your office
needs. Won't you call me for an interview?

Yours truly,

Craig Allen

Craig Allen

Anticipating reasons for rejection

As part of your take-charge job-search strategy, you will want to anticipate anything that might prevent your being interviewed and try to neutralize it in the application letter. In almost every instance, you will be submitting a resume with your application letter. Is there anything on the resume (a medical problem, an arrest or prison record, failure in school, a history of too many jobs held for too short a time) that might cause an employer to reject you? If so, you will have to handle the problem in your letter.

Of course, you could just omit any damaging information from your resume. And, in many cases, that is the wisest thing to do. The resume doesn't have to include *every* piece of information about you. Indeed, it can't. If you were fired from a job, for example, you shouldn't say so on the resume, although you may have to discuss the matter at the interview. Just omit the "reason for leaving" category in the work history section of your resume. No one is perfect, and the resume is not a confession of errors. It is intended to show what's *good* about you.

In Chapter 4, you saw how William Smith camouflaged his less-than-impressive work history by using a functional rather than a chronological resume. This is legitimate and a credit to Smith's marketing skills. It is not legitimate, however, to lie on a resume or in an application letter. Nor is it in your interests to ignore glaring flaws in your background. Sooner or later, you will have to deal with them, either at the interview or after you get the job.

If you have some major factor in your background that will definitely work against your getting the job or might cause the employer to dismiss you after you're hired, it's probably best to tackle it head-on in the letter. Take a look at these two sample paragraphs:

Although, as my resume shows, I am well qualified for the position, you should know that I was fired from my last job. The circumstances were complicated, but I was asked to leave because I was caught taking company property from the supply room. I don't consider myself a thief, and I have no criminal record. This was an isolated case of poor judgment, and it's not something I am proud of. I'll be happy to discuss the details of this incident with you at my interview, but I thought you should know this fact about me ahead of time. I'm eager to work for you and want our relationship to begin on a solid, honest basis.

The enclosed resume will give you additional information about my background; what it won't tell you is that I am blind as the result of a hunting accident twelve years ago. My disability has not stopped me from traveling—I went to England with a friend last year—or from working. I have been employed and supporting myself since I left high school. Although I am sure that my blindness will not influence your judgment regarding my qualifications for the position of social services counselor, it can make some people a little uneasy until they get to know me.

You have probably heard the old saying "Honesty is the best policy." In these two examples, the writers have probably impressed their readers by the courage and honesty they displayed in confronting a difficult topic directly.

Recasting negative factors in positive language

In most cases, the reason for a possible rejection won't be as dramatic as the two examples just presented. But most people have something in their background that could work against their getting a particular job. In assessing your qualifications, remember that no situation is totally black or white. A woman returning to paid employment after taking time away from the workplace to raise her children doesn't need to apologize for her outdated skills, for example. Instead, she can emphasize the wisdom and maturity she can offer over younger candidates; she can indicate that she will have fewer of the distractions younger people might have if they are raising children. A young man with little or no work experience can promote himself as "eager to learn," and a person who has had a number of jobs can offer an employer "wide experience," "flexibility," or "a knowledge of various work environments and types of people." It's a matter of stating the negative in positive terms, seeing the proverbial glass of water as half-full rather than half-empty.

Your turn

Rewrite the following negative statements from job applicants in positive terms. After you have finished, compare your rewrites to those at the end of the chapter.

1. As you can see from my resume, I worked part-time as a long-distance truck driver for Ace Transportation Company, but I have been out of work for about six months. To make ends meet, I have been doing some light hauling around town, using my own truck.

    _____

    _____

    _____

    _____

    _____

    _____

    _____

2. I have a degree in drafting, but I had to take a job on construction until something opened up in my field.

    _____

    _____

    _____

    _____

_____

_____

_____

3. I hope you'll consider my application even
   though I don't have a college degree. I had to
   drop out of school because of illness, and I
   was limited in the work I could do. Most of
   my experience is just as a volunteer at St.
   Mary's Hospital where I am manager of the
   gift shop.

_____

_____

_____

_____

_____

_____

_____

   In today's wide and rapidly changing job market, the applicant's qualifications may well be outdated or not exactly on target for the job in question. In such cases, it is necessary to show how experience or training in
one field can be applied to another field. Take a look at the sample application letter on the next page and notice how the applicant has tried to "sell"
her liberal arts educational background to an employer who is looking for
someone with a business degree. Knowing her application may be rejected
the minute the employer spots the liberal arts background on her resume,
the writer is taking some risks with the tone and content of her letter. Is the
letter effective? Would you interview this person?

   Because Como is applying for a position for which she believes she is
qualified but for which she does not have the "official" qualifications—in
this case, a degree in business—she is trying to secure special attention for
her application by writing a somewhat flamboyant application letter. In effect, she demonstrates in her application letter her ability to write—the
actual task she will be doing on the job—and minimizes the fact that she
does not have the kind of degree specified in the company's ad.

   As an exercise, imagine you are applying for a job outside your field.
What other kinds of work _could_ you do with your background, skills, and
interests? How would you present your qualifications?

5659 Pine Ridge Road
Greeley, Colorado 80634
July 7, 1989

Mr. Walter G. Lockhart
Promotion Department
Columbia Insurance Company
117 Seventh Ave.
Denver, Colorado 80211

Dear Mr. Lockhart:

I have a good sense of humor, but I never understood a popular joke that circulated at the University of Colorado when I was a student there. "What are you studying," one student was supposed to have asked another. "Nothing," the second student replied, "I'm in Liberal Arts."

As a Liberal Arts student, I guess I was a little defensive. It seemed that most of the good jobs were going to students in business. But since I graduated in 1987, I've had a number of opportunities to use the reasoning and writing skills I learned as a Liberal Arts student. I didn't study "nothing" in school. I learned to think and respond effectively in a number of personal and work environments.

My ability to write, for example, allowed me to work as an advertising agency copywriter for two years with Addison and Farley of Denver. There I had to be able to master quickly the vocabulary, philosophy, and manner of speaking of diverse account clients. I wrote about dairy products and automobile parts, but because I had learned as a Liberal Arts student the study skills necessary to tackle any new field of knowledge, I found that I could produce good copy on each new product or service I wrote about.

I know the ad in Sunday's Post specifies a person with a degree in business for the position of promotional writer at Columbia Insurance, but won't you let me discuss my unique qualifications with you in person? I know I can learn the insurance business quickly and write about it effectively in your company publications. And I think after you have looked over my resume and talked with me, you will agree that my flexibility and background can be very useful to you in the Promotion Department. I'll telephone next week to see about setting up an appointment.

Sincerely,

Susan Como

Discussion of chapter exercises

Opening paragraphs for unsolicited application letters, page 96

1. This is a well-written opening paragraph. The hook that establishes a relationship between writer and reader is credible and shows that the writer is truly interested in real estate investment. The tone is informal but not too personal.

2. Applying for a permanent job at a firm where you have worked on a part-time basis is a good job strategy; the hook here is credible. But this writer's tone is too friendly. Whether or not Riggs was a great guy is beside the point, and the statement that the work was "easy and paid well" doesn't present the writer in the best light. The final sentence is vague and lacks enthusiasm.

3. The hook here is nothing specific, just the writer's admiration for the reader's company. That's fine as an opening-paragraph strategy, but the tone in which this admiration is expressed may be too flattering. The writer is clearly exaggerating in the first sentence. Notice, too, the word choices: "impossible," "highly successful," "inspiration." If this tone seems heavy-handed to you, how would you rewrite it to suit your own tastes?

Model application letters, pages 100–102

Van Patton (p. 100) probably isn't worth interviewing. Although he *seems* as though he might have the qualifications for the job, he doesn't make much of an effort to *prove* it to the employer. The opening paragraph is vague and lifeless; the body of the letter fails to give specific information, and the concluding paragraph takes a kind of "wait and hope" attitude rather than attempting to nail down an interview. Notice, too, that the letter isn't centered on the page, and there are a number of format errors (no zip code in the heading, incorrect punctuation after the salutation, no consistency in whether "Michigan" is spelled out or abbreviated in the addresses). Finally, the spelling errors ("alot," "truely") mark the letter as unacceptable.

The format of Morton's unsolicited application letter (p. 101) is correct (she uses a full-block, open-punctuation style), and the opening paragraph strikes a nice tone. The information presented is credible and relates to the job Morton wants. The second paragraph, although it doesn't mention a specific job, does make it clear what the letter is about.

The second half of the letter seems to go off track, however. The third paragraph begins well, with the writer showing how her background *particularly* qualifies her for the job. The mention of a particular research interest is a good strategy, too, because if Morton is interviewed, she and the interviewer will have something specific to talk about—something Morton can discuss impressively.

But the latter half of the paragraph brings in an unexplained personal element. The second sentence should have ended with the word "substitutes." Instead, it rambles on, stumbling into awkwardness. Further, the reader may be made uneasy by the final sentence because it's difficult to know how the remark about "very personal reasons" ought to be interpreted.

Finally, the fourth paragraph fails to ask for a specific action. How should it read? Would you interview this applicant? If so, what would you ask her, based on her letter?

There is only one format error in Allen's letter (p. 102): his name should not appear in the heading. The letter reads smoothly and contains lots of specific, relevant information. The only question is the tone. Given the nature of the job for which he is applying, is Allen being *too* breezy? What about the opening sentence? Does it insult Mr. Goldstein by telling him something he already knows, or does it show awareness of what's happening on the campus? Is the tone too boastful in the final paragraph? Whether or not you like the tone of this letter says something about you. Certainly, a letter like Allen's makes an impression—unlike Van Patton's letter. Allen is confident and enthusiastic. Would you interview him? Why or why not?

Recasting negative factors in positive language, pages 104–105

1. You may have heard someone say that the best way to get a job is to look as though you don't need one. Well, it's true. If you seem desperate, pitiful, or defeated, you may make employers so uncomfortable that they won't want to deal with you. Here, the phrases "out of work" and "to make ends meet" convey a negative picture of the applicant. No matter how bad things are, present yourself as positive, optimistic, and in control of your life. Suggested rewrite:

> With the extensive experience I gained as a
> long-distance truck driver for Ace Transportation
> Company, I was able to start my own light
> hauling business.

2. This writer is a victim, someone reacting to economic circumstances rather than controlling his or her career moves. Since the construction job is relevant to drafting, why not represent it as a *choice* rather than as a matter of necessity? For example:

> After I received my degree in drafting, I
> decided to get some first-hand experience in the
> construction industry. As a carpenter with White
> Construction, I learned a lot about how
> blueprints become homes; and I think I'm a
> better draftsman for the experience.

3. Never "hope" in a job application letter; it's not a take-charge attitude. And never apologize for credentials you don't have. Finally, never bring your personal life into the job-search process unless you have to. Here, depending on the circumstances, the writer may have to explain the absence of an extensive work history; but the explanation should not represent the applicant as a victim. If you must make a difficult personal statement in your letter to explain aspects of your resume, do it as briefly as possible: "Unfortunately, illness prevented me from completing school." Or minimize the personal statement by stating it in a dependent clause: "When illness forced me to leave school, I. . . ."

Look again at this paragraph. The writer has failed to recognize positive aspects about his or her background. Managing a shop is solid business experience, whether or not the job is a paying one. Most people tend to underrate their own experience and overrate the experience of others. Think about your own background. Have you overlooked skills and experience hiding in minor jobs or hobbies?

To an extent, employers treat your background the same way you do. If you minimize its significance, so will they. Notice in the following rewrite that the volunteer position is described as "work" — which it certainly is — and the duties of the job are explained at length, turning a possibly negative element into a positive one.

When illness prevented me from finishing my degree in sociology, I found challenging work as a hospital volunteer. My job as Gift Shop Manager at St. Mary's Hospital requires me to handle purchase orders and manage a staff of five people in addition to waiting on customers and balancing cash register receipts.

part IV The job interview

10 Anticipating the interview

Every job interview is different. Some interviewers want you to do all the talking; some hardly let you say a word. Some like putting you on the spot to see how you react to pressure, and some try to put you at ease. Interviews vary not only because interviewers have differing ideas as to what an interview should reveal, but also because some interviewers are more skillful than others. It's hard to believe, but some interviewers are almost as nervous at the interview as you are.

To meet any possible interview situation, you must be well prepared and eager to talk about your qualifications. Think through the interview ahead of time, and try to anticipate what will happen. What is the interviewer likely to ask you, and what would be an appropriate and impressive response? What do you want to get out of the interview?

The purpose of interviews

Unfortunately, most people look upon the job interview as an interrogation, an opportunity for the potential employer to grill the applicant, searching out flaws and shortcomings. If you think of the interview that way, it's likely to be that way. Those who expect the interview to be stressful put stress on themselves long before the interviewer has a chance to do so.

Of course, the job interview is a little more tense than a relaxed evening with close friends, but it's not the fact that the interviewer asks questions or even the fact that the interviewer has the power to accept or reject the applicant that makes the interview stressful. Rather, it's the fact that most applicants take a passive role in the interview process. Once you agree to be "done to" rather than act, you put yourself in a helpless, vulnerable position. You look—and probably feel—like someone waiting for the worst to happen—a pitiful victim rather than an attractive potential employee.

Think of the people you know. Those you like to be with are probably outgoing and lively. They don't expect you to do all the talking or make all the decisions. There is a sense of sharing in your encounters with these people. The same personal dynamics are at work in a job interview. If you sit, silent and passive like so much dead weight, you can't blame the interviewer for wanting to dismiss you as soon as possible.

Stop and ask yourself why the interview is taking place. Why were you called in? Why is the interviewer taking time to talk with you? After all, your qualifications are on the resume, and most companies have or could prepare company job application forms to gather any information the resume doesn't include. The employer could check your references for an objective opinion of your abilities. What's happening at the interview beyond the mere gathering of objective information?

The answer is that the interview is more than a chance for the employer to gather information about you; it's an opportunity for you to *perform* and for the employer to see first-hand how well you can manage a situation. You are being asked to *act* so that the employer can make judgments based not on the facts of your resume but on how you look, how you speak, how well you can think on your feet. Yes, these judgments will be somewhat subjective, but that needn't be a disadvantage to you if you understand what is going on and agree to take an active role in the interview process.

The first step in "acting out" the job interview is to look upon it as a conversation with someone who has knowledge on a subject in which you are interested. In this sense, all interviews are "research" interviews, situations in which your goal is to gather information rather than secure a job offer. It may be difficult to imagine at this point, but there will be jobs you won't want, just as there will be employers who won't want you. Like the employer, you will want to evaluate how well your abilities and aspirations match the company's requirements. Would this job challenge you, give you opportunities to advance? Your goal in the interview is not only to present your qualifications effectively, but to find out as much as possible about the job and the company—in effect, to interview the interviewer. Don't go into the interview with the attitude that you *must* get the job. You will want to make sure the job is right for you before you take it.

Staying in control

Assuming the role of both applicant *and* interviewer may, at first, seem overwhelming. It may even seem a bit presumptuous. Acting as the interviewer does have the advantage, however, of giving you a measure of control over the interview situation. Of course, you won't take over. The employer will still be in charge. But having the goal of securing information—that is, an active goal—rather than passively waiting to be accepted or rejected, will do a great deal to calm your nerves. This, in turn, will help you present your qualifications in the best light.

As with any anticipated conversation, you will want to think ahead of time about what you and the interviewer can talk about. Of course, you will have checked your school's placement office and library for information on the company (see Chapter 2). But what else can you do beforehand to make the interview a success?

Think of the interviewer almost as a blind date or a visiting relative you must entertain. What do you have in common? What does he or she need to know about you? What can you ask the interviewer about the company he or she represents? Remember the service attitude. What can you do to help the interview go smoothly *for the interviewer?*

Talking about yourself

Control, especially self-control, is a delicate balance. It's easy to become rattled early in the interview, in which case you may never recover your composure. To make sure this doesn't happen, think through short, informal responses to general questions like the following before you arrive at the interview:

■ What sort of job are you looking for and why?
■ Why did you choose the field you did?
■ What are you hoping to do in the future?
■ Why are you interested in this particular company?
■ What is your educational background? What courses did you study and what did you learn from them?

These questions are the type often used to begin an interview. Don't memorize a formal speech, but be ready to speak regarding your background and why you are applying for the particular position. Prepare both a concise, fifteen-second answer and a longer, more detailed response. At the interview, use the response that seems more appropriate, judging by the style and pace the interviewer sets.

Some interviewers will take control of the interview immediately and talk a while before they ask you anything. Some will ask you a series of short-answer questions: "Where did you go to school?" "When did you graduate?" "How did you learn of this job?" But some will simply throw the ball to you with an open-ended invitation to talk: "Tell me a little bit about yourself." If you can't respond coherently and at length to this challenge, you will certainly lose points with the interviewer—and perhaps your composure as well.

Like most people, you probably grew up with the idea that talking about yourself is impolite. Even statements of fact such as "I earned high grades in college" or "I have a definite aptitude for math" sound like bragging. You may also have developed the habit of minimizing your accomplishments, diverting attention from yourself so as not to seem conceited. It's hard to talk about yourself in positive terms, but that's exactly what the job interview demands of you.

In talking about yourself, it's helpful to remember that the job interview is a special situation, a unique personal encounter, and that in talking about yourself in a job interview you are simply fulfilling the demands of the situation. Remember, too, that statements of fact about yourself do not constitute bragging. Stick to the facts and you'll feel more comfortable.

Planning what to say

To get yourself in the habit of talking positively about yourself, use the space here to list three accomplishments of which you are particularly proud:

1. _____

2. _____

3. _____

After each accomplishment, write what that accomplishment indicates about you as a person. For example, if you went to night school to get your high school diploma after dropping out of school, you showed perseverance. If you are a volunteer firefighter, you show a commitment to your community and a willingness to sacrifice to help others.

Now, try putting your impressive personal quality and the accomplishment that demonstrates that quality together in a sentence: "My _____(accomplishment)_____ shows that I am _____(quality)_____."

1. _____

_____

2. _____

_____

3. _____

_____

Next, list three abilities you have that might be of value to an employer (for example, the ability to type, repair office equipment, deliver speeches, drive a large van or truck, operate special equipment):

1. _____

_____

2. _____

_____

3. _____

_____

Think of a job in which each ability would be useful, and put the ability and the job title together in a specific, positive statement: "As a _____(job title)_____ for your firm, my ability to _____(ability)_____ would be especially useful."

1. _____

   _____

2. _____

   _____

3. _____

   _____

The statements you have just written probably sound pretty mechanical, but they are just "limbering-up" exercises, ways to help you see how you can make specific positive statements about yourself based on evidence from your background. You won't be reciting these statements to an employer, but you probably will have to make some sort of extended statement about yourself.

In Chapter 3, you did some thinking and writing about yourself and your goals. Go back and read what you wrote. Now, suppose an interviewer has just asked you to discuss your background and goals. On the next page, outline what you would say. (You will, no doubt, repeat here some of the ideas you used in Chapter 3, as well as add some new thoughts. That's okay. The more practice you have in discussing yourself in positive terms, the better.)

CAREER GOALS

_____
_____
_____
_____
_____
_____
_____
_____
_____
_____
_____
_____
_____
_____
_____
_____
_____
_____
_____
_____
_____
_____
_____
_____
_____
_____
_____

Interview questions that ask you to evaluate yourself

Most interviews will include a few questions that ask you to evaluate yourself, questions like the following. In the space provided, indicate how you would respond. Write complete sentences.

1. What are your strengths; that is, what personal qualities make you a good worker? _____

_____

_____

_____

_____

2. What are your weaknesses? _____

_____

_____

_____

_____

3. Why did you choose the field you did? _____

_____

_____

_____

_____

4. Where do you hope to be and what do you hope to be doing five years from now? _____

_____

_____

_____

_____

5. What is your idea of success? _____

_____

_____

_____

_____

Anticipating other general question areas

Of course, you cannot anticipate exactly what questions an interviewer might ask or how they might be phrased, but you can anticipate the general areas that will be explored: educational background, work experience, aspirations, personal life (marital status, hobbies, health). You should have all the facts regarding your educational and work background in mind before you go to the interview: dates of schooling and employment, employer's address and telephone number, supervisor's name, duties performed, salary, grade point average, and so forth. Even though it's your life story, it is easy to forget details about your work and educational history. Take a copy of your resume to the interview along with photocopies of the work and educational history forms you completed in Chapter 3 and any additional notes in your employment file; you may need these facts to fill out a company employment application form.

Be ready, too, to evaluate your work and educational history and to answer such questions as: "What courses did you enjoy most in college and why?" "What did you learn on the job?" "What would you do differently if you were starting college all over again today?"

Undoubtedly, you will be asked about your aspirations: "What do you hope to accomplish?" "What ultimate job are you aiming toward?" Answer questions about your goals as specifically as possible to show that you have thought about your career and have formed some definite plans. Then add, if possible, something a bit more "philosophical." Don't be vague and sentimental about wanting to "serve humanity" and "do good in the world," but don't be afraid to talk about ambitions beyond a solid job and a good paycheck. Be sincere.

Inappropriate and trick questions

Some employment counselors make much of the fact that employers have no business asking applicants certain personal questions, questions such as: "Do you plan to have children?" "Why were you divorced?" "Do you attend church?" It's true that questions about your race, religion, political affiliation, or personal life are out of line—and, in many cases, illegal—but before you become visibly offended, ask yourself how much answering them will really cost you. Interviewers usually have good reasons—or, at least, believe that they have good reasons—for asking the questions they do. Some may be prejudiced or just curious, but some may simply not be aware that certain questions are offensive or illegal. As individuals, job applicants respond to interview questions differently, and much depends on circumstances. If you believe you have been treated unfairly, however, and you wish to pursue the matter, you should seek legal advice.

Often, you can answer a question evasively with a statement such as "I hadn't really thought much about that" or "I don't anticipate that my personal life will interfere with my work." Another good strategy is to answer the question with another question: "How does that relate to the job?" Or: "Why do you ask?" If you really don't want to answer a question, say so frankly, but without hostility: "I would rather not go into my personal life." A good response to a question that is too personal is to return the discussion to the job: "My divorce is in the past. I'd rather concentrate now on my future in electronic engineering." If you handle an awkward situation tactfully and frankly, most interviewers will admire you for it.

Some interviewers are straightforward; others have "tactics"—tricky questions designed to surprise you, test you, or put you under stress. An interviewer may walk briskly into the room, shake your hand, and ask, "What can I do for you?" The question ignores the fact that he or she *knows* why you are there and instead transfers control of the situation to you. Be prepared to state the obvious: "I'd like to discuss my qualifications for the position of parts department manager which was advertised in Sunday's *Tribune*."

The surprise question is designed to test how well you think on your feet and how well you can control a situation. If, despite your attempts to anticipate all possible aspects of the interview, a question genuinely surprises you and you have no answer, say so: "I'm sorry, I just don't know how to answer that. I'd have to give the matter a little more thought." A frank and sincere response can be impressive.

Some interviewers like to probe for flaws and shortcomings in your background: "Why did you leave your last job?" "Why weren't you working during the summer last year?" "Why didn't you take more advanced math in college?" Sometimes this probing can be aggressive: "You're a little underqualified for this position, aren't you?"

Often the interviewer is attempting to determine how you stand up under criticism. The best response when you feel yourself under attack is to admit whatever truth there is in the accusation, then turn the situation so that it reflects well on you. If you have genuine flaws in your background (you failed courses, you were fired from a job), never lie. Admit your mistake (nobody's perfect) and go on to say what you learned from it: "Yes, I'm sorry to say I was fired by Ray's Conoco Station, but I learned a lot from the experience. I think it forced me to grow up and develop a better sense of responsibility. I've been in my present job for almost two years now, and my employer seems happy with my work."

The question of salary

One final area of possible questioning concerns salary. Having researched the employment area in which you are applying, you should have some idea of what the job in question probably pays. But you should also have calculated your expenses. What is the least amount of money you must earn to pay your rent, car expenses, charge accounts, and food bills? Know both what you need and what to expect in the way of salary before you go to the interview. If and when the employer asks you what you would expect to earn, deflect the question: "I'm not so much concerned with my initial salary as with my chances for advancement." Or: "Salary is less important to me than the opportunity to work in a major company like Allied and gain experience. I'm sure that starting salaries at Allied are competitive." If the employer insists that you give a figure, name a salary range, not a specific amount. Don't ask for an unrealistic salary on the presumption that companies offer as little as possible; but don't be too humble either. Know what is fair.

Rehearsing for the interview

Interviewing gets easier the more interviews you do, so you don't want an important interview to be your first. Practicing ahead of time is a good idea. Get a friend to act as the employer and ask some questions from the following list. If you don't have a specific job in mind, make one up or find one in the classified advertising section of the newspaper. Try to formulate brief, specific answers. If you can't find someone to help you conduct a mock interview, go through the list alone and plan your answers. Respond to the questions out loud. It's easy in reading a question over to *think* you know how you would answer it; it's another thing entirely to have to put your answer in words. The first few responses you make will probably be fumbling and confused. Go over the questions again and again until you are used to the sound of your own voice answering them and you are satisfied that your answer is clear and impressive. Strive to be brief, positive in tone, specific, and sincere.

1. Why are you interested in this particular job?
2. What course work did you complete in college that seems relevant to this particular job?
3. Have you done similar work before? Where? What were your duties?
4. What are your strengths and weaknesses?
5. Tell me a little bit about your family background.
6. What are your hobbies? How did you get interested in them? Why do you enjoy them?
7. If you got this job, what would you do first?
8. Do you feel there are gaps in your education, areas in which you don't feel confident?
9. How well do you take criticism?
10. What do you feel is the best way to manage people?
11. What is your pet peeve?
12. Why did you choose the college you did?
13. How would you rate your school among others?
14. What, in your opinion, would be the ideal job?
15. What do you hope to be doing five years from now?
16. What salary would you expect to receive to start?
17. Do you feel the grades you received in school accurately reflect your ability? Why or why not?
18. What do you feel sets you apart from other applicants with the same educational background?
19. Whom do you admire most and why?
20. Don't you think you're being too ambitious in applying for this job?

Preparing questions to ask

If you want to impress the interviewer, you must take an active role in the interview. You must show that you understand what the job will entail and that you are interested in it. This means asking questions. At a certain point in almost every job interview, the employer will invite you to ask questions. Have some ready.

The questions you ask will, of course, depend on the job situation, but here are a few *not* to ask:

— What does this job pay? (You'll find out when and *if* you get a job offer. Don't give the impression that money is all you care about.) Most companies have established salary categories. If the interviewer mentions a salary, don't react either negatively or positively. Don't try to negotiate a higher figure.

— How much vacation do I get? (Again, you haven't gotten the job yet, so it's too early for you to need a vacation. Act on the assumption that the company treats its employees fairly.)

■ How long will I have to work at this job before I'm promoted? (*If you get the job, you'll have to prove yourself first in order to earn advancement.*)

All of these questions center on what is of benefit to the applicant, not on what the applicant can do to help the employer. Remember the service attitude. And remember, too, that at the interview stage, you haven't gotten the job yet.

Instead of asking what's in it for you, concentrate on demonstrating your knowledge of the company and your sterling qualities: intelligence, enthusiasm, initiative. Study the company beforehand, just as you would study for a test at school. Know something about its history, philosophy, future plans. Here's the kind of question you should be planning to ask:

■ Locating in the Midwest must increase the firm's shipping costs. What does the company gain by being located here in Omaha?
■ How will the new EPA regulations affect the Denver plant?
■ I read that Blackwell is planning to introduce a new line of office equipment designed for the home. What is the thinking behind that decision?

These are general examples, but you get the idea. Questions about the company's philosophy, history, products and services, standing in the marketplace, and future plans are all in order. Make up about a dozen specific questions and practice asking them before the interview. Make the questions "real," that is, inquiries to which you really want answers. In other words, present yourself as well informed but eager to learn. As an applicant, you aren't supposed to know all the answers, but you are expected to be able to ask an intelligent question.

Interview situations for discussion

Here are some typical interview questions and imagined responses that will help you formulate your own responses to anticipated interview questions. Keeping in mind that a good response is brief, upbeat in tone, specific, and sincere, evaluate the responses as though you were the interviewer. Which candidates would you reject? Which might you hire? After you have considered these responses, turn to the discussion of them at the end of the chapter.

1. INTERVIEWER: Well, Mr. Rinehart, tell me a little about yourself.
   CANDIDATE: Well, there's not much to tell. I graduated from Fairview College this spring, and I'm looking for a job. I saw your ad in the paper.
2. INTERVIEWER: What sort of position were you looking for?
   CANDIDATE: I don't really know. I'm willing to do anything.
3. INTERVIEWER: Why did you leave your last job, Dave?
   CANDIDATE: The boss and I just didn't see eye-to-eye. He was a real maniac about details, a real fussy guy. I'm not like that. I figure, if the job gets done, who cares how it gets done? So, one day, he told me I had to put back all the tools right after I used them instead of at the end of the day—that's how we always used to do

it, just pick everything up at the end of the day, unless, of course, we were going to need the same tool in the morning. He had this big rack made for all the tools with labels telling what went where. Anyway, he said, pick them up; and I said, no way. So I just walked off the job.

4. INTERVIEWER: Tell me about your husband. How does he feel about your working? Won't your children miss their mommy?
CANDIDATE: I don't think any of that concerns you.

5. INTERVIEWER: What courses did you take at Fairview, Mr. Jennings?
CANDIDATE: Oh, just the usual liberal arts courses. The curriculum is pretty much the same for everyone. I did take some drama courses, though.

6. INTERVIEWER: What were your duties on your last job, Beverly?
CANDIDATE: I was called the Public Relations Director. The title is a little bit fancy for what I really did. I worked for a hospital, but only on a part-time, free-lance basis—forty hours a month—writing their newsletter. The job involved not only interviewing physicians and other hospital personnel and writing up stories, but taking all the photographs for the newsletter, too. I was also responsible for planning lobby displays and advising the media of activities at the hospital.

7. INTERVIEWER: Your transcript shows you failed freshman English and had to repeat the course in summer school. Frankly, Miss Grant, that concerns me because this job calls for some writing.
CANDIDATE: When I started attending Fairview, I planned to work about thirty hours a week in addition to going to school. As the transcript shows, this was too much for me to handle. So, when I began my sophomore year, I cut my work back to fifteen hours, and as you can see, my grades improved. I think students should work their way through school; it develops character. Incidentally, I took several English electives in my junior and senior years, including a course in creative writing, and did well in them.

Discussion of chapter exercises

Interview questions and responses, pages 123–124

1. By refusing to talk, the candidate here has thrown away a golden opportunity to score points in the interview. Mr. Rinehart is completely passive, and the interviewer is going to have to drag the information out of him. He should have said something like this:

> Well, I'm a recent graduate of Fairview College in hotel and restaurant management, and I'm looking for a position as a management trainee. I saw your ad in Sunday's *Tribune* for an assistant manager, and I wanted to discuss my qualifications with you. As you can see from my resume, I have worked in restaurants for the past five years.

This sort of response indicates that Mr. Rinehart knows what he is doing. He has taken an active role in the interview and assured the interviewer that their time together will be pleasant and productive.

2. No one is really "willing to do anything" (peel potatoes, scrub down the kitchen floor with a toothbrush?). Here, the candidate is leaving all the work to the interviewer. Job applicants should know the name of the job for which they are applying. Suggested response:

> I am looking for a position as a field representative for a major book publisher. I would prefer to sell college textbooks, but I would accept a position with a trade publishing house, too.

3. If you even considered hiring this candidate, don't go into business for yourself. His response indicates he is uncooperative and disorganized and doesn't know when to stop talking. A candidate should never say uncomplimentary things about a former employer. If the relationship was unpleasant, try to put the most positive face on it you can. For example: "It was simply one of those personality clashes that happens from time to time. I enjoyed my work, but eventually, it seemed better for all concerned if I sought employment somewhere else." Better yet, use a secondary reason for leaving: "I felt I had learned all I could from that job, and I wanted to try something new."

4. The interviewer should not have asked this question, but the candidate here is too abrupt. It's possible that the interviewer is being condescending, but it's also possible that he or she is trying to show a warm interest in the candidate's family. Don't risk misreading the interviewer's message and overreacting. Just say something neutral such as: "My husband and I have talked the matter over, and I don't anticipate that my family life will interfere with my work."

5. Another golden opportunity missed! The candidate should be trying to separate himself from the herd, not telling the employer his credentials are just like everyone else's. Also, the employer doesn't necessarily know what the "usual" liberal arts courses are. Always be specific in answering interview questions like this one. For example: "I majored in history with a particular concentration of courses in British history, but I also took a number of business courses, including accounting, management, retailing, and advertising. I took an acting course just for fun, and I found it gave me a lot more confidence in my sales work and public speaking."

6. This candidate is being specific, but she is also belittling the work she did—a common mistake. Just give the facts and let the interviewer decide whether or not your credentials are impressive: "I was the Public Relations Director on a part-time basis. I worked forty hours a month, writing the hospital newsletter. This involved interviewing physicians, administrators, and staff members; writing; and buying print. I took all the photographs for the newsletter, too, and I planned special displays and promotions in consultation with the Administrator."

7. This candidate is doing fine—admitting a fault honestly, then going on to show how she corrected it. But what about her remark that students should work their way through school? Would this statement impress you if you were the interviewer? Why or why not?

11 Handling the interview

From the reading you have done so far, you know that being knowledgeable about the company and taking an active role in the interview are important. But until you have actually interviewed, you may not realize just how important preparation is or exactly how to use your preparation to impress the interviewer. The more you interview, the more you will realize how much you need to prepare. You'll get better at interviewing—more skillful, less nervous—the more interviews you have.

This being the case, it's smart to do a few "practice" interviews first. If you are working with your college placement center, try to set up appointments with campus recruiters in an ascending order of importance so that your "dream" job is not the first one for which you interview. Practice working through the job-search process by applying for jobs listed in the newspaper. This will not only help you polish your interviewing skills, it will also help you make contacts and get a sense of what is available in your field. Obviously, it is a waste of everyone's time, including your own, for you to apply for jobs for which you are not qualified or jobs you wouldn't consider accepting. Choose realistic possibilities, but try to leave the best for last. By the time you are scheduled for the "big" interview, you'll have done extensive preparation and you will have had plenty of practice in taking charge.

It's natural to be nervous at a job interview; and if you control your nerves, that extra pressure may even help you do well. The best way to control nerves is to be well prepared: organized, armed with information, and confident that you look the part of a promising candidate.

What to take to the interview

In addition to having thought about yourself and your qualifications and having thoroughly researched the company to which you are applying, being prepared means having everything you need to apply when you show up for the interview. Here's a checklist of items you should bring with you:

- Two extra copies of your resume (in case the interviewer wants to pass them along to other people in the organization)
- A copy of your school transcript (The employer may want to have this in your file. It will also remind you of specific courses you took.)
- A neatly typed list of your references to give to the employer (name, title, business address, and business telephone number for each reference)
- Prepared questions to ask the interviewer (just to refresh your memory and show the interviewer that you *do* have questions prepared)
- Organized information regarding past jobs, former addresses, and education to use in filling out company application forms (These forms often ask for specific dates, salary, supervisor's name, address, and telephone number of former places of employment. Photocopy the work and educational histories you completed in Chapter 3 and take them with you to the interview.)
- Notes from your research of the company and any company literature you have collected (to show the interviewer that you *have* done some homework)
- Samples of your past work if appropriate
- Your social security card, driver's license, work permit, union card, or whatever legal documentation you may need
- A pen and some paper

You don't need a hundred-dollar briefcase to be impressive; just a crisp file folder with these items organized in it.

Image

At first thought, it may seem as though your whole life will be open for examination at a job interview, and that's bound to make anyone nervous. That's why it's important to realize that in an interview you are presenting not the total you, but an image. You are presenting your professional self; and although that self is really you and not a phony, it's only a part of you, the part you want to show.

You may like to smoke or chew gum, for example, but don't smoke or chew gum during the interview. That's a part of yourself you don't want to show the interviewer—not because it's "wrong" to smoke or chew gum, but because it's a leisure activity. It doesn't fit the occasion or the professional image you are presenting. Likewise, you may be a staunch Republican, a devout Catholic, a supporter of hand-gun control, an anti-vivisectionist. Keep those facets of yourself private, not because the interviewer may hold different views, but because those issues aren't part of your professional image. They don't relate to the job and your qualifications for it, so they don't belong in the interview.

The same is true of your shortcomings. Ignore them. Your professional image consists of what you can do, not what you can't. As for any past failures, those are called "learning experiences." Everyone has had them. Rather than worrying over general questions (Will the interviewer like me? Am I good enough to work for the company?), concentrate on the specific, positive aspects of the professional image you are building, beginning with your appearance.

Appearance

At first, it may seem unfair that employers judge applicants by their appearance, but think about how many times a day you make inferences about people from the way they look. Appearances can be deceiving; but taken along with other evidence, they can also reveal information about a person's character, status, and attitudes. There are exceptions, of course; in general, however, people's clothing and grooming standards reflect the way they see themselves and the way they wish others to think of them. The man wearing the Ralph Lauren polo shirt is making a statement about himself. So is the man wearing the Harley Davidson tee-shirt.

Companies are teams on which every member is trying to make the same statement. This doesn't mean that every employee has to look and think like every other. But, in general, employers are seeking people who "look like" they will fit in.

Interviewing isn't a beauty contest, and you won't lose out on a job because the interviewer doesn't like the color of your tie. But pay attention to grooming: clean hair, clean fingernails, and so on. An employer is not going to want you on the team if your standards of personal hygiene don't match the company image.

As for clothing, you don't need to buy an expensive new outfit to interview, nor do you need to confine your dress to somber colors and severely conservative styles. Just use your common sense and avoid obviously inappropriate dress: tennis shoes or running shoes rather than leather shoes, gaudy jewelry, loud colors, high-powered colognes or perfumes, tee-shirts with slogans printed on them, clothing better suited for dates and parties than business occasions, clothing clearly designed for recreational wear, or any item that calls attention to itself.

Ideally, the interviewer should not be particularly aware of what you are wearing. After all, you want him or her to remember you, not your suit. If you are in doubt as to what to wear, stop by the company ahead of time and observe the people who work there. Copy their dress.

One good rule of thumb is to dress slightly better than you would on the job if you were actually employed by the company. If you are applying for a job on the loading dock, for example, you need not wear a three-piece suit to the interview, but you shouldn't wear jeans either, even though you would probably dress in jeans on the job. A nice pair of slacks and a sport shirt for men or a basic skirt and blouse for women are usually fine for applying for jobs in which you will be wearing a uniform or jeans. For office and professional-level jobs, both men and women should probably interview in business suits.

Details

Sometimes applicants get so involved with the major concerns of the interview that they forget to take care of the details. For example, learn the name of the interviewer beforehand, if possible—and how to pronounce it (if it's an unusual name, ask the secretary or the interviewer how it should be pronounced). If you are given your interview appointment verbally, repeat it to make sure you have understood correctly. Write down the time, date, and address; file the information in your employment file or write it in your appointment book.

Telephone the day before to confirm your appointment. Doublecheck the address and be sure you know how to find it and how long it will take you to get there. Arriving late or failing to show up for an interview almost guarantees you won't get the job. If, due to *extraordinary* circumstances, you must cancel an interview or you find you will arrive late, telephone the interviewer's office and explain.

Attitude

The image-building pointers discussed so far in this chapter—how to dress, what to take with you to the interview—are really just strategies for demonstrating your attitude toward yourself, the employer, and the job you want. Undoubtedly, there are people working today who did not remember to take a pen with them to the interview or interviewed in tennis shoes or mispronounced the interviewer's name. Interviewing isn't a sacred ritual in which every detail is defined and must be executed precisely. It's a human encounter, which means that it is not so much what you do as the attitude you reveal that counts. Being prepared *shows* that your attitude is positive—that you want the job and are willing to work to get it.

Likewise, taking an active role in the interview demonstrates that you are enthusiastic, but it also shows that you have the skills and intelligence to manage a situation, present your qualifications effectively, and ask pertinent questions.

Some applicants go into the interview with the attitude that it's the interviewer's job to ask the questions. Employers, these applicants believe, know what they are looking for, and they will tell the applicant whatever he or she needs to know.

This fatalistic approach might make sense if employers hired only a grade point average or a set of credentials. But employers hire *people,* human beings with personalities, goals, and character traits. Your resume alone won't show that you are ambitious or hard-working or friendly. You must demonstrate that by taking an active part in the interview—by talking and listening.

Strategies for demonstrating your personality

You don't have to tap dance on the desk to show you have personality, but it wouldn't hurt to smile. Here are a few more strategies to help you break through the formality of the interview and establish yourself as an individual.

Responding to your environment

Too often, interviewers have to pry information from nervous job applicants. That's why it's a good strategy to say something beyond "Hello" when you meet the interviewer. It need not be profound, just an everyday pleasantry, some indication that you are alive and confident and ready to participate in the interview.

When you get to the site of the interview, look around you; take notice of the office and the people in it; check out the pictures on the wall. Is there anything to which you can respond? You don't want to rattle on, but a brief personal comment can help you relax and seem more confident than you may actually be. Sports and the weather are traditional small-talk topics, but it really doesn't matter what you say. The important thing is to say something to signal the interviewer that the interview will be a lively exchange, not a forced march.

Asking questions and listening

You should have some general questions prepared ahead of time (see Chapter 10), but the most impressive questions will be those you ask in response to what the interviewer says. That's why it's important to *listen*.

There is nothing more flattering to a speaker than knowing that someone is listening carefully. Leaning forward a little, maintaining eye contact, and nodding now and then to indicate comprehension are all gestures actors and actresses use to show that a character is paying close attention to a speaker. You can use them, too, without being phony. They are just additional ways to communicate.

Most people aren't able to concentrate well enough to listen. It takes practice. Don't pretend to listen. Concentrate. Imagine that you will be tested later in the interview on what the interviewer has said. In a way, you will be; and you will certainly lose points if you failed to "hear" the information given you. To make sure you understand what the interviewer is telling you, ask for clarification. For example: "Could you give me an example, please? I want to be sure I understand what you are saying." Or: "In other words, you are saying that. . . ."

Volunteering information

You are the "seller" in an interview. That means you can't just wait and hope that the interviewer asks the right questions about you. You have to volunteer information in order to make sure that the interviewer learns of your best selling points. For example: "I'd like to tell you more about my work as a student counselor because I think it demonstrates my ability to work with people." Or: "My course work at Colson College included more lab work and practical, hands-on training than most academic institutions offer. I'd like to outline what the program was like because I think it relates specifically to the kind of work I'd be doing for you."

By taking an active role and volunteering information, you will not only ensure that the interviewer learns impressive information about you; you will also demonstrate that you know your worth and can take charge of a situation.

Pointers

Here are a few more interviewing tips to remember:

1. Greet the interviewer by name, and tell him or her your name. Yes, the interviewer *knows* your name, but announcing yourself is a mark of confidence and good business manners.
2. If the interviewer offers to shake your hand, give him or her a firm—not a crushing—handshake.

3. Follow the interviewer's lead. You are the guest in this situation, so wait for the interviewer to invite you into the office; wait for him or her to invite you to sit down.

4. Sit up straight. Leaning back in the chair may indicate an arrogant attitude; hunching forward may suggest you are nervous. Look the interviewer in the eye. Hanging your head will make you look timid; looking around the room will suggest that you are not focused on the interview. Maintaining eye contact is important, but don't engage in a relentless staring contest with the interviewer.

5. Try not to squirm or fidget. Fold your hands in your lap.

6. The first five minutes of an interview are the most critical; that's when the interviewer is forming a lasting first impression of you. Respond at length to early questions, if possible. You should have prepared yourself to speak on general questions regarding your background and goals. An impressive initial response will give you confidence and make a good first impression on the interviewer. Try not to answer *any* question with only a yes or a no unless such an answer is the only appropriate response.

7. To check how you are doing, watch the interviewer's reactions. Be aware of the pace of the interview. If there are long pauses after each question, your answers may be too brief. If the interviewer breaks eye contact with you, checks the time, or shuffles papers, your answers probably are too long.

8. React to what the interviewer says. Express interest, smile, ask a question, or make a brief, appropriate remark. Try to break the mood of interrogation that interviews sometimes have by making your tone slightly conversational.

9. At the end of the interview, express interest in the position and thank the interviewer for the opportunity to present your qualifications.

10. Don't take notes during the interview; it's distracting for the interviewer. But do jot down what was said as soon as possible after you leave. Keep notes on every interview to use later in following up.

Recovering a fumble

There is such a thing as "chemistry," and because of chemistry, an interviewer may take a dislike to you for no good reason. Or you may dislike the interviewer. This doesn't happen often with professional people—that's part of what makes them professional—but it does happen. Misunderstandings can occur.

The minute you detect that something is going wrong, take action to correct the tone. If the interview seems to be going off course, if hostilities are surfacing, or if you and the interviewer seem to be talking at cross-purposes, it is best to confront the situation quickly and directly rather than let the interview degenerate further. You could say something like this: "I don't seem to be communicating very well in response to your questions. Perhaps it would be better if I just outlined my work history for you." Or: "I feel I may not be making myself clear—I'm a little nervous, I guess. What I meant to say was. . . ."

It's okay to show that you recognize something has gone wrong, and it's definitely right to try to repair any damaged feelings or to clear up any misunderstandings. Being sensitive to personal interactions and being able to correct awkward situations—"people skills," as these abilities are sometimes called—are valuable assets in the business world. But don't go overboard with your sensitivity. Keep your statement brief, and be willing to accept the blame; then go on: "I'm afraid I may have said something to offend you. If so, I apologize. The point I was trying to make was . . ."

Questions for discussion

1. How would you describe the appearance of ideal male and female job candidates in your field? If you were an employer hiring workers in your field, what aspects of a candidate's appearance might cause you to reject him or her? Be specific.

2. Think of someone in your field who you think has a good professional image. Describe that person, listing four or five specific character traits.

3. Is it phony or dishonest to consciously present a business "image" at an interview? What is the difference between the "real" person and the image? Can you think of analogies to the business image? In what other situations might people decide to reveal only a part of themselves? Why would they choose to do so?

12 Following up

As you learned in the previous chapter, you should conclude a job interview with a clear and enthusiastic expression of your interest in the job—if you *are* interested. It is legitimate, too, to ask tactfully what your chances are; but be sure not to seem overly confident or too eager, and don't press the point if the interviewer seems reluctant to answer. Before you leave the office, you should also ask the interviewer when you might expect to learn his or her decision regarding your application (the interviewer will usually tell you this; but if not, ask). Depending on the circumstances, you might even want to offer to telephone the interviewer for the decision.

All of these strategies are designed not only to demonstrate your competence but also to help you stay in charge. The job-search process isn't over when the interview ends, and you will want to continue to try to influence the employer's decision rather than let yourself be stranded in a "wait and hope" situation.

The follow-up letter

To continue to sell yourself as a lively, enthusiastic candidate, you will need to write at least one follow-up letter. However unflattering it may be to realize it, your face and resume will probably fade quickly from the interviewer's mind unless you reinforce the impression you made with some sort of action. That's what follow-up letters are intended to do: remind the interviewer of what was said during your interview and, thus, fix you and your qualifications in the interviewer's memory.

Your first follow-up letter will almost always be a formal thank-you letter expressing your appreciation for the opportunity to present your credentials. It's only polite, after all, to thank someone who spent time and effort on your behalf. But a follow-up letter that does no more than say thank you is not likely to make a lasting impression. As in the unsolicited application letter, you will need to find a "hook," that is, some *specific* additional reason for the letter.

A good hook is something specific that the interviewer advised and you followed up on: a recommended book, a source of information, a contact. If you are clever, you can even "plant" a hook at the time of the interview by asking for information or referrals. This establishes a relationship between you and the interviewer, a reason for you to contact the interviewer again. For example:

> Thanks for taking time recently to talk with me about job openings at Farley Inc. Incidentally, I contacted Joe Moran in Personnel as you advised, and he was able to give me the information on internships that I asked about during the interview.

Here, the letter recalls something specific from the interview, something that sets the candidate apart from all the others. Further, it tells the interviewer that the candidate listened to what the interviewer said and followed up on it. In effect, the candidate is demonstrating traits that will make him or her a good employee.

Some applicants intentionally "forget" to mention an important credential or reference during the interview as an excuse to write the employer again. If you are not good at acting, however, forget that strategy and simply pick out something you learned in the interview and comment on it. Try to say something specific and memorable, not: "Your discussion of the plant's recent security problems was very interesting." Conclude your letter with a restatement of your interest in the job.

Take a look at the letter on the following page and notice how the writer has used specific details to follow up on something discussed at the interview. Notice, too, that the writer expresses a strong interest in the company. Too often, applicants just let the employer *assume* they are interested in the job.

Turning down a job

Sometimes the participants at an interview discover that there just isn't a match between applicant and employer. In a roundabout way, that's good. Applicants lose time and, sometimes, confidence when they go into jobs that aren't right for them; employers lose money when they hire people who don't work out.

If you are not impressed with a firm—or sense that people there are not impressed with you—don't show it. You can't afford to burn your bridges behind you. The business world is a network of people talking to other people, and you want everyone—including the interviewer you didn't especially like—to be talking positively about you. Even if the interview was a disaster, write a brief, positive follow-up letter. And if you like what you learned about a company at the interview, say so.

On the other hand, if there is a match and you receive an offer, ask for time (a week or so, depending on circumstances) to think it over. Interviews are stressful occasions, and you may be too rattled to evaluate the offer clearly. If, after some thought, you do decide to turn down a job offer, don't just telephone. Take time to write an impressive letter to the employer. Nothing is forever, and if the rapport was good between you and the interviewer,

1929 Forty-fifth St.
St. Louis, MO 63112
April 19, 1989

Mr. J. D. Kellerman
Production Manager
Beta Products Incorporated
99 Weston Road
St. Louis, MO 63110

Dear Mr. Kellerman:

First, let me thank you for taking time to visit with me
yesterday regarding career opportunities at Beta Products. Your
company's literature had given me a good sense of Beta's history
and philosophy, but talking with you clarified a number of
questions I had regarding the company's current role in the food-
processing industry.

I'm especially grateful to you for mentioning the Andrew Lewis
article on careers in microbiology. I read it in the university
library and was amazed to learn how many options people with my
background have in organizations such as yours.

As I mentioned to you, I'm hoping to be able to tour Beta some
time soon and talk with your production microbiologists. What I
have learned so far about the company's plans for the future
convinces me that I very much want to be a part of your growing
organization.

Sincerely,

Vincent W. Porter

hang on to it. You may be able to use the interviewer to make contacts with other employers; or a better, more interesting job may turn up with that same company in the future. Be sure to thank the employer for his or her consideration and indicate that you gave the matter serious thought. Say something positive. For example:

> I thought a long time about the position you offered me at our last meeting. Working with the technicians at Webster/Starkey would be excellent practical experience. But, as I mentioned to you, I want to relocate in the East, and I have decided to accept an offer from a company in Delaware. Thank you again for considering me.

Being turned down

When applicants fail to impress an interviewer, it's usually because they:

- Were not prepared for the interview
- Demonstrated no knowledge of the company
- Seemed indecisive about career goals and abilities
- Lacked enthusiasm and motivation
- Presented a poor appearance

If you "blow" an interview for one of these reasons, you'll probably realize it the minute you leave the office, if not before. Pay attention to the reactions of the interviewer and the tone and pace of the interview. If there are long pauses, you are probably not volunteering enough information. If the interviewer asks you questions about the firm that you should be able to answer but can't, you need to do more research. The more you interview, the better you will become in analyzing and improving your performance.

Building a career is a life-long process in which you do not so much *succeed* in your field as *become successful*. In other words, success is a process, not an occasion. Thus, if you are rejected as underqualified, read that rejection not as a permanent "no" but as a "not right now" reaction to your qualifications. Make notes about what the interviewer said and use them as a basis for reapplying to the company later. In the meantime, write a follow-up letter that will keep the door open. For example:

> I appreciate the honest advice you gave me when we talked last Monday. Although I'd like to go to work for your firm tomorrow, I understand that to be valuable to you, I'll need to gain more practical experience first. Thanks for taking the time to interview me. When I've had more experience, I hope we can talk again about career opportunities at your firm.

Persistence

Don't give up. If you really want to work for the company, ask the employer to keep your resume and correspondence on file. Then try them again in six months with another follow-up letter, but make that letter reflect a stronger, better-qualified candidate than the one the company turned down earlier. In other words, show that you are moving ahead in your career, not stalled.

Again, you must have a hook—a reason for writing, something to catch the reader's attention. This can be news of recent accomplishments and added credentials, an updated resume, or simply a reaffirmation of your interest in the company. Take a look at the letter on the next page. Notice that the writer doesn't beg for a job, but she does make it clear that she still wants to work for the company.

57 Amis Drive, Apt. 4
Santa Fe, NM 87501
December 6, 1989

Mrs. Martha Grey
Personnel Director
First Financial Group
701 Third Ave.
Santa Fe, NM 87510

Dear Mrs. Grey:

As you may remember, I talked with you last summer about an opening at First Santa Fe Financial Group as an investment accounting trainee. I had just graduated from college then, and you advised me to get more business and accounting experience before attempting to move into this specialized area.

Since we talked, I have taken a job as an accountant with Newell-Eisley. In this position, I am able to apply my accounting degree to practical everyday business situations. Under the direction of Henry Eisley, Jr., I analyze ledger expense accounts and prepare memos and worksheets for use in preparation of the annual statement, and I have helped conduct internal auditing functions.

I know that at Newell-Eisley the office staff cleans out the files around this time of year. If that is the policy at First Financial Group, won't you please keep my correspondence and resume in your active file so you can notify me when another trainee position opens up. I am still very interested in working for First Financial, and I think a second interview would convince you that I am ready for the challenge of this position.

Yours truly,

Mary Lee Harper

Mary Lee Harper

Reassessing yourself and your job-search strategies

You can't expect to get a job offer every time you interview; but if you have been looking for work for three months or more without success, you should reassess yourself and your job-search strategies.

Begin by troubleshooting your resume. Does it look good on the page? Are you using quality paper? Have you misspelled any words? Is the information complete and detailed enough? Are you using a chronological format when a functional format might serve you better? Experiment with the format, the typography, and the manner of presentation. If the resume seems too crowded, cut it down. If it seems skimpy, expand it.

Next, look carefully at the application letters you've been sending out with your resume (remember, always keep a copy of every letter you send). Do they seem like "form" letters, or is each one tailored to a specific job? Do they "sell" you by highlighting impressive credentials from the resume? Do they reflect a service attitude? Is the tone appropriate?

Try writing in a style as different as possible from the one you have been using. If you have been writing formal letters, for example, try to write a more personal one. Compare your new style with the old. Ask a teacher, a business person, or someone in the placement office to read over your letters and resume and give you an honest reaction.

Get some honest opinions, too, on yourself and the way you interview. Most college placement offices will coach you on interviewing; some even have video equipment that will enable you to see for yourself how you come across in an interview. Talk to professors you know well, and ask them to evaluate your communication skills. Ask them how they would describe you and what traits of yours impress or annoy them. Because professors observe a number of people in your same circumstances, they can help you see how you compare to others. Further, most of them have a genuine interest in helping students succeed.

Finally, you may need to reexamine your goals in relation to your qualifications. Are you aiming too high? Do you need to get additional training or gain more experience before you can compete for the job you want? If so, exactly what must you do to upgrade your qualifications? Would you be more successful in another part of the country? Are there company training programs or internships for which you might be eligible? Are there jobs less related to your field that might offer a place to start? Again, business people, teachers, and counselors in the placement office can help you sort through your options.

Once you have reassessed your goals and the means you have devised to sell your qualifications and reach those goals, reactivate and expand your contact network. The teachers, friends, and business people you contacted when you began your job search will, by now, probably have new names and additional information to give you. Don't hesitate to reapply to a company; your persistence will mark you as determined and confident. Explore new ways to think about yourself and your abilities. Stay flexible and optimistic.

index

Abbreviations, 56
Abilities, 29, 33, 37, 42, 51
  analyzing, 20, 48-49
Active role
  in job search, 4, 10, 11, 91
  vs. passive, 4, 17
Appearance, for job interviews, 129
Application letter
  appearance of, 99
  body of, 90-91
  conclusion of, 91
  function of, 85-86, 95
  invited, 95
  models of, 100, 101, 102, 106
  opening of, 89-90, 92-93, 95-96,
    107
  reassessing, 140
  unsolicited, 95-96
Aspirations, 5
  talking about, 120. *See also* Goals
Attention line, 74, 77
Attitude, 130

Body, of business letter, 74, 76,
    86-87, 92. *See also* Application
    letter
Business letters
  appearance of, 73-74
  models of, 75, 78, 79, 81, 88
  organization of, 86-87, 89, 92
  parts of, 74, 76-77, 80
    See also Application letter

Career statement essay, 33-35
Closed punctuation. *See* Punctuation
Company evaluation form, 15-16
Company literature, 9, 10, 11-13
Competition, 4
Complimentary close, of business
    letter, 74, 76

Conclusion, of business letter, 86, 87,
    92. *See also* Application letter
Connections, 8. *See also* Contacts,
    network of
Consistency, 55-56
Contacts, network of, 10-11, 140
Control, maintaining, 114-15
Convention, 73-74
Copies, of letters, 12-13
Copy notation, 77-80
Cover letter. *See* Application letter

Depth of presentation, 51, 57-58, 61,
    63-64
Detail
  in follow-up letter, 136
  in resume, 56, 57, 58-59, 63, 69
Dun & Bradstreet, 13
Duties, enumeration of, 19-20, 57,
    68, 69

Educational history, 19, 29, 33, 41,
    51, 52, 57, 64, 119-20, 128
  recording of, 25-28
Emotionalism, 99
Emphasis, 63
  and order of presentation, 52
Employment agencies, 17-18
Enclosure notation, 74, 77
Experience, lack of, 104
Extracurricular activities, 49, 57, 63

Failure, reasons for, 138
File system, 11-13, 36
First impression, 52, 58, 68, 132
Follow-up letter
  after rejection, 136, 138
  as thank you letter, 135-36
  models of, 137, 139
Forbes, 14

Fortune, 14
Full-block indentation. *See* Indentation

Goals, 29, 51
    clarifying, 9, 33
    reassessing, 140
    See also Job objective

Hanging indentation, 63, 68, 69
Heading
    of business letter, 74
    in resumes, 62, 63, 64, 68, 69
    second page heading, 76
Hook, in business letter writing, 96,
    107, 136, 138

Image, 51, 128-29
Indentation, 42
    forms of in business letters, 80
Initials, of typist and dictator, 77
Inside address, of business letter, 74,
    76
Interest, importance of expressing,
    3-4, 91, 132, 135, 136
Interview. *See* Job interview
Interviewers, 113
    studying reactions of, 132, 138
    tactics of, 115, 120-21

Job interview, 13, 115
    asking for, 91
    preparing for, 113, 114, 115-23,
        127, 129-30
    pointers for, 131-32
    purpose of, 113-14
    questions asked at, 29, 115, 119,
        120-21, 122
    questions candidates ask at, 122-23
    taking an active role in, 113-14,
        122, 124, 127, 130-31
Job objective, as part of resume, 48,
    59, 62, 69
Job offer, turning down a, 136-38

Listening, importance of, 131, 136

Manner of presentation, 51, 55-57,
    61, 62-63
Mixed punctuation. *See* Punctuation
Modified-block indentation. *See*
    Indentation

Newspaper ads, 12, 17
Nonwork experience, 48-49, 57-58,
    108-9

Notes
    importance of, 13, 128
    taking, 13, 15, 132, 138

Open punctuation. *See* Punctuation
Opening, of business letter, 86, 92.
    See also Application letter
Order of presentation, 51-55, 61, 62

Parallelism, 56
Persistence, 138
Personal data, 58, 63, 65, 68
    as section of resume, 42, 62, 69
Persuasion, 3, 86, 90
Photographs, 36, 64
Placement office, 9-10, 12, 13, 114,
    127, 138
Postscript, 80
Prospecting letter. *See* Application
    letter, unsolicited
Punctuation, 55, 56, 63, 82-83, 97

*Readers' Guide to Periodical
    Literature,* 13
References, 36, 62, 64, 65, 69, 128
Referrals, 10, 14, 136
Rejection
    anticipating reasons for, 103-4
    handling, 138
Researching
    companies, 13-14
    job market, 9-13
Research interview, 14-15, 114
Resume
    appearance of, 41, 56-57
    chronological, 41-42, 47-49, 51-55,
        61, 140
    format of, 51-60
    functional, 41-42, 47-49, 51-55,
        59, 61, 64, 140
    general requirements of, 41, 61
    models of, 43-46, 54, 60, 66-67
    pointers for writing, 61-64
    reassessing, 140
    as work, 51
Reverse chronology, 42, 52, 62, 90

Salary, 62
    avoiding mention of, 8, 64
    discussing at interview, 121
Sales campaign, job search as, 4-5,
    19, 41, 131, 140
Sales letter, 85-86, 87
    model of, 88
Salutation, of business letter, 74, 76

Self-analysis, 5, 29-33
  as part of resume writing, 51
Semi-block indentation. *See*
    Indentation
Sequence, of information on resume,
    55, 62-63
Service attitude, 5-7, 65, 74, 86, 87,
    90, 91, 115, 123, 140
Shotgun technique, 17
Signature block, of business letter,
    74, 76
Standard and Poor's Register of
    Corporations, Directors and
    Executives, 13
Stationery, 41, 74
Style, writing, 56
  experimenting with, 140
  formal and informal, 97-98
  of magazine and newspaper
    articles, 52

  in resume writing, 56, 63, 68
  word choice in, 8, 56, 98, 107
Subject line, 77
Supporting documents, 36-37

Thomas' Register, 13
Tone, 89, 96-99, 105, 140
Transcripts, 14, 36, 128
Typography, 56-57, 58, 63, 68, 69,
    140

Voice, active vs. passive, 97, 99

Wall Street Journal, 14
Work history, 29, 33, 41, 47-49, 51,
    52, 57, 64, 119-20, 128
  recording of, 19-24
Work samples, 36-37, 128
Writing style. *See* Style, writing

WE VALUE YOUR OPINION—PLEASE SHARE IT WITH US

Merrill Publishing and our authors are most interested in your reactions to this textbook. Did it serve you well in the course? If it did, what aspects of the text were most helpful? If not, what didn't you like about it? Your comments will help us to write and develop better textbooks. We value your opinions and thank you for your help.

Text Title _____ Edition _____

Author(s) _____

Your Name (optional) _____

Address _____

City _____ State _____ Zip _____

School _____

Course Title _____

Instructor's Name _____

Your Major _____

Your Class Rank _____ Freshman _____ Sophomore _____ Junior _____ Senior

_____ Graduate Student

Were you required to take this course? _____ Required _____ Elective

Length of Course? _____ Quarter _____ Semester

1. Overall, how does this text compare to other texts you've used?

_____ Superior _____ Better Than Most _____ Average _____ Poor

2. Please rate the text in the following areas:

	Superior	Better Than Most	Average	Poor
Author's Writing Style	_____	_____	_____	_____
Readability	_____	_____	_____	_____
Organization	_____	_____	_____	_____
Accuracy	_____	_____	_____	_____
Layout and Design	_____	_____	_____	_____
Illustrations/Photos/Tables	_____	_____	_____	_____
Examples	_____	_____	_____	_____
Problems/Exercises	_____	_____	_____	_____
Topic Selection	_____	_____	_____	_____
Currentness of Coverage	_____	_____	_____	_____
Explanation of Difficult Concepts	_____	_____	_____	_____
Match-up with Course Coverage	_____	_____	_____	_____
Applications to Real Life	_____	_____	_____	_____

3. Circle those chapters you especially liked:
   1   2   3   4   5   6   7   8   9   10   11   12   13   14   15   16   17   18   19   20
   What was your favorite chapter? _____
   Comments:

4. Circle those chapters you liked least:
   1   2   3   4   5   6   7   8   9   10   11   12   13   14   15   16   17   18   19   20
   What was your least favorite chapter? _____
   Comments:

5. List any chapters your instructor did not assign. _____

6. What topics did your instructor discuss that were not covered in the text?_____

   _____

7. Were you required to buy this book? _____ Yes   _____ No

   Did you buy this book new or used? _____ New   _____ Used

   If used, how much did you pay? _____

   Do you plan to keep or sell this book? _____ Keep   _____ Sell

   If you plan to sell the book, how much do you expect to receive? _____

   Should the instructor continue to assign this book? _____ Yes   _____ No

8. Please list any other learning materials you purchased to help you in this course (e.g., study guide, lab manual).

   _____

9. What did you like most about this text? _____

   _____

10. What did you like least about this text? _____

    _____

11. General comments:

    May we quote you in our advertising? _____ Yes   _____ No

    Please mail to: Boyd Lane
                      College Division, Research Department
                      Box 508
                      1300 Alum Creek Drive
                      Columbus, Ohio 43216

    Thank you!